J. T. (John Townsend) Trowbridge

The Man Who Stole a Meeting-House and Preaching for

Selwyn

J. T. (John Townsend) Trowbridge

The Man Who Stole a Meeting-House and Preaching for Selwyn

ISBN/EAN: 9783337004682

Printed in Europe, USA, Canada, Australia, Japan

Cover: Foto ©ninafisch / pixelio.de

More available books at **www.hansebooks.com**

THE MAN WHO STOLE A MEETING-HOUSE

AND

PREACHING FOR SELWYN

BY

J. T. TROWBRIDGE

AUTHOR OF "CUDJO'S CAVE" "THREE SCOUTS"
"NEIGHBOR JACKWOOD" ETC. ETC.

BOSTON
LEE AND SHEPARD PUBLISHERS
10 MILK STREET
1897

Norwood Press:

Berwick & Smith, Norwood, Mass , U.S.A.

THE MAN WHO STOLE A MEETING-HOUSE.

ON a recent journey to the Pennsylvania oil regions, I
stopped one evening with a fellow-traveller at a village which had just been thrown into a turmoil of excitement by the exploits of a horse-thief. As we sat around
the tavern hearth, after supper, we heard the particulars
of the rogue's capture and escape fully discussed; then
followed many another tale of theft and robbery, told
amid curling puffs of tobacco-smoke; until, at the close of
an exciting story, one of the natives turned to my travelling acquaintance, and, with a broad laugh, said, " Kin ye
beat that, stranger ?"

" Well, I don't know, — maybe I could if I should try.
I never happened to fall in with any such tall horse-steal-
ing as you tell of, but I knew a man who stole a meeting-
house once."

" Stole a meetin'-house ! That goes a little beyant anything yit," remarked another of the honest villagers. " Ye
don't mean he stole it and carried it away ?"

" Stole it and carried it away," repeated my travelling
companion, seriously, crossing his legs, and resting his arm
on the back of his chair. " And, more than all that, I
helped him."

" How happened that ? — for you don't look much like a
thief, yourself."

All eyes were now turned upon my friend, a plain New

England farmer, whose honest homespun appearance and candid speech commanded respect.

"I was his hired man, and I acted under orders. His name was Jedwort, — Old Jedwort, the boys called him, although he was n't above fifty when the crooked little circumstance happened which I 'll make as straight a story of as I can, if the company would like to hear it."

"Sartin, stranger! sartin! about stealin' the meetin'-house!" chimed in two or three voices.

My friend cleared his throat, put his hair behind his ears, and with a grave, smooth face, but with a merry twinkle in his shrewd gray eye, began as follows : —

" Jedwort, I said his name was; and I shall never forget how he looked one particular morning. He stood leaning on the front gate, — or rather on the post, for the gate itself was such a shackling concern a child could n't have leaned on 't without breaking it down. And Jedwort was no child. Think of a stoutish, stooping, duck-legged man, with a mountainous back, strongly suggestive of a bag of grist under his shirt, and you have him. That imaginary grist had been growing heavier and heavier, and he more and more bent under it, for the last fifteen years and more, until his head and neck just came forward out from between his shoulders like a turtle's from its shell. His arms hung, as he walked, almost to the ground. Being curved with the elbows outward, he looked for all the world, in a front view, like a waddling interrogation-point enclosed in a parenthesis. If man was ever a quadruped, as I 've heard some folks tell, and rose gradually from four legs to two, there must have been a time, very early in his history, when he went about like Old Jedwort.

" The gate had been a very good gate in its day. It had even been a genteel gate when Jedwort came into possession of the place by marrying his wife, who inherited it

from her uncle. That was some twenty years before, and
everything had been going to rack and ruin ever since.

"Jedwort himself had been going to rack and ruin,
morally speaking. He was a middling decent sort of man
when I first knew him ; and I judge there must have been
something about him more than common, or he never
could have got such a wife. But then women do marry,
sometimes, unaccountably. I've known downright ugly
and disagreeable fellows to work around, till by and by
they would get a pretty girl fascinated by something in
them which nobody else could see, and then marry her in
spite of everything ; — just as you may have seen a mag-
netizer on the stage make his subjects do just what he
pleased, or a black snake charm a bird. Talk about women marrying with their eyes open, under such circumstances ! They don't marry with their eyes open : they
are put to sleep, in one sense, and a'n't more than half re-
sponsible for what they do, if they are that. Then rises
the question that has puzzled wiser heads than any of ours
here, and will puzzle more yet, till society is different from
what it is now, — how much a refined and sensitive woman
is bound to suffer from a coarse and disgusting master,
legally called her husband, before she is entitled to break
off a bad bargain she scarce had a hand in making. I've
sat here to-night, and heard about men getting goods under false pretences ; you've told some astonishing big sto-
ries, gentlemen, about rogues stealing horses and sleighs ;
and I'm going to tell you about the man who stole a meeting-house ; but, when all is said, I guess it will be found
that more extraordinary thieving than all that often goes
on under our own eyes, and nobody takes any notice of it.
There's such a thing, gentlemen, as getting hearts under
false pretences. There's such a thing as a man's stealing
a wife.

"I speak with feeling on this subject, for I had an opportunity of seeing what Mrs. Jedwort had to put up with from a man no woman of her stamp could do anything but detest. She was the patientest creature you ever saw. She was even too patient. If I had been tied to such a cub, I think I should have cultivated the beautiful and benignant qualities of a wild-cat; there would have been one good fight, and one of us would have been living, and the other would have been dead, and that would have been the end of it. But Mrs. Jedwort bore and bore untold miseries, and a large number of children. She had had nine of these, and three were under the sod and six above it when Jedwort ran off with the meeting-house in the way I am going on to tell you. There was Maria, the oldest girl, a perfect picture of what her mother had been at nineteen. Then there were the two boys, Dave and Dan, fine young fellows, spite of their father. Then came Lottie, and Susie, and then Willie, a little four-year-old.

"It was amazing to see what the mother would do to keep her family looking decent with the little means she had. For Jedwort was the tightest screw ever you saw. It was avarice that had spoilt him, and came so near turning him into a beast. The boys used to say he grew so bent, looking in the dirt for pennies. That was true of his mind, if not of his body. He was a poor man, and a pretty respectable man, when he married his wife; but he had no sooner come into possession of a little property than he grew crazy for more. There are a good many men in the world, that nobody looks upon as monomaniacs, who are crazy in just that sort of way. They are all for laying up money, depriving themselves of comforts, and their families of the advantages of society and education, just to add a few dollars to their hoard every year; and

so they keep on till they die and leave it to their children,
who would be much better off if a little more had been in-
vested in the cultivation of their minds and manners, and
less in stocks and bonds.

"Jedwort was just one of that class of men, although
perhaps he carried the fault I speak of a little to excess.
A dollar looked so big to him, and he held it so close, that
at last he could n't see much of anything else. By degrees
he lost all regard for decency and his neighbors' opinions.
His children went barefoot, even after they got to be great
boys and girls, because he was too mean to buy them
shoes. It was pitiful to see a nice, interesting girl, like
Maria, go about looking as she did, while her father was
piling his money into the bank. She wanted to go to
school and learn music, and be somebody ; but he would n't
keep a hired girl, and so she was obliged to stay at home
and do housework ; and she could no more have got a dollar out of him to pay for clothes and tuition, than you
could squeeze sap out of a hoe-handle.

"The only way his wife could ever get anything new
for the family was by stealing butter from her own dairy,
and selling it behind his back. 'You need n't say anything to Mr. Jedwort about this batch of butter,' she
would hint to the storekeeper ; 'but you may hand the
money to me, or I will take my pay in goods.' In this
way a new gown, or a piece of cloth for the boys' coats, or
something else the family needed, would be smuggled into
the house, with fear and trembling lest old Jedwort should
make a row and find where the money came from.

"The house inside was kept neat as a pin ; but everything around it looked terribly shiftless. It was built
originally in an ambitious style, and painted white. It
had four tall front pillars, supporting the portion of the
roof that came over the porch, — lifting up the eyebrows

of the house, if I may so express myself, and making it look as if it was going to sneeze. Half the blinds were off their hinges, and the rest flapped in the wind. The front doorstep had rotted away. The porch had once a good floor, but for years Jedwort had been in the habit of going to it whenever he wanted a board for the pig-pen, until not a bit of floor was left.

"But I began to tell about Jedwort leaning on the gate that morning. We had all noticed him; and as Dave and I brought in the milk, his mother asked, 'What is your father planning now? Half the time he stands there, looking up the road; or else he's walking up that way in a brown study.'

"'He's got his eye on the old meeting-house,' says Dave, setting down his pail. 'He has been watching it and walking round it, off and on, for a week.'

"That was the first intimation I had of what the old fellow was up to. But after breakfast he followed me out of the house, as if he had something on his mind to say to me.

"'Stark,' says he, at last, 'you've always insisted on 't that I wasn't an enterprisin' man.'

"'I insist on 't still,' says I; for I was in the habit of talking mighty plain to him, and joking him pretty hard sometimes. 'If I had this farm, I 'd show you enterprise. You wouldn't see the hogs in the garden half the time, just for want of a good fence to keep 'em out. You wouldn't see the very best strip of land lying waste, just for want of a ditch. You wouldn't see that stone-wall by the road tumbling down year after year, till by and by you won't be able to see it for the weeds and thistles.'

"'Yes,' says he, sarcastically, 'ye 'd lay out ten times as much money on the place as ye 'd ever git back agin, I 've no doubt. But I believe in economy.'

"That provoked me a little, and I said, 'Economy! you're one of the kind of men that 'll skin a flint for sixpence and spoil a jack-knife worth a shilling. You waste fodder and grain enough every three years to pay for a bigger barn, — to say nothing of the inconvenience.'

"'Wal, Stark,' says he, grinning and scratching his head, 'I've made up my mind to have a bigger barn, if I have to steal one.'

"'That won't be the first thing you've stole, neither,' says I.

"He flared up at that. 'Stole?' says he. 'What did I ever steal?'

"'Well, for one thing, the rails the freshet last spring drifted off from Talcott's land onto yours, and you grabbed : what was that but stealing?'

"'That was luck. He couldn't swear to his rails. By the way, they 'll jest come in play now.'

"'They've come in play already,' says I. 'They've gone on to the old fences all over the farm, and I could use a thousand more without making much show.'

"'That's 'cause you're so dumbed extravagant with rails, as you are with everything else. A few loads can be spared from the fences here and there, as well as not. Harness up the team, boys, and git together enough to make about ten rods o' zigzag, two rails high.'

"'Two rails?' says Dave, who had a healthy contempt for the old man's narrow, contracted way of doing things. 'What's the good of such a fence as that?'

"'It'll be,' says I, 'like the single bar in music. When our old singing-master asked his class once what a single bar was, Bill Wilkins spoke up and said, "It's a bar that horses and cattle jump over, and pigs and sheep run under." What do you expect to keep out with two rails?'

"'The *law*, boys, the *law*,' says Jedwort. 'I know

what I 'm about. I 'll make a fence the *law* can't run under nor jump over; and I don't care a cuss for the cattle and pigs. You git the rails, and I 'll rip some boards off 'm the pig-pen to make stakes.'

" ' Boards a'n't good for nothin' for stakes,' says Dave. ' Besides, none can't be spared from the pig-pen.'

" ' I 'll have boards enough in a day or two for forty pig-pens,' says Jedwort. ' Bring along the rails and dump 'em out in the road for the present, and say nothin' to nobody.'

" We got the rails, and he made his stakes; and right away after dinner he called us out. ' Come, boys,' says he, ' now we 'll astonish the natives.'

" The wagon stood in the road, with the last jag of rails still on it. Jedwort piled on his stakes, and threw on the crowbar and axe, while we were hitching up the team.

" ' Now, drive on, Stark,' says he.

" ' Yes; but where shall I drive to?'

" ' To the old meetin'-house,' says Jedwort, trudging on ahead.

" The old meeting-house stood on an open common, at the north-east corner of his farm. A couple of cross-roads bounded it on two sides; and it was bounded on the other two by Jedwort's overgrown stone wall. It was a square, old-fashioned building, with a low steeple, that had a belfry, but no bell in it, and with a high, square pulpit and high, straight-backed pews inside. It was now some time since meetings had been held there; the old society that used to meet there having separated, one division of it building a fashionable chapel in the North Village, and the other a fine new church at the Centre.

" Now, the peculiarity about the old church property was, that nobody had any legal title to it. A log meeting-house had been built there when the country was first settled and land was of no account. In the course of time that was torn down, and a good framed house put up in its place. As it belonged to the whole community, no title, either to the house or land, was ever recorded; and it was n't until after the society dissolved that the question came up as to how the property was to be disposed of. While the old deacons were carefully thinking it over, Jedwort was on hand, to settle it by putting in his claim.

" ' Now, boys,' says he, ' ye see what I 'm up to.'

" ' Yes,' says I, provoked as I could be at the mean trick, ' and I knew it was some such mischief all along. You never show any enterprise, as you call it, unless it is to get the start of a neighbor. Then you are wide awake; then you are busy as the Devil in a gale of wind.'

" ' But what *are* you up to, pa?' says Dan, who did n't see the trick yet.

" The old man says, ' I 'm goin' to fence in the rest part of my farm.'

" ' What rest part?'

" ' This part that never was fenced; the old meetin'-house common.'

" ' But, pa,' says Dave, disgusted as I was, ' you 've no claim on that.'

" ' Wal, if I ha'n't, I 'll make a claim. Give me the crowbar. Now, here 's the corner, nigh as I can squint '; and he stuck the bar into the ground. ' Make a fence to here from the wall, both sides.'

" ' Sho, pa!' says Dan, looking bewildered; ' ye a'n't goin' to fence in the old meetin'-house, be ye?'

" ' That 's jest what I 'm goin' to do. Go and git some big stuns from the wall, — the biggest ye can find, to rest the corners of the fence on. String the rails along by the road, Stark, and go for another load. Don't stand gawpin' there !'

" ' *Gawpin'* ?' says I; ' it 's enough to make anybody

gawp. You do beat all the critters I ever had to deal with. Have n't ye disgraced your family enough already, without stealing a meeting-house?'

" ' How have I disgraced my family?' says he.

" Then I put it to him. 'Look at your children; it's all your wife can do to prevent 'em from growing up in rags and dirt and ignorance, because you are too close-fisted to clothe 'em decently or send 'em to school. Look at your house and yard. To see an Irishman's shanty in such a condition seems appropriate enough, but a genteel place, a house with pillars, run down and gone to seed like that, is an eyesore to the community. Then look at your wife. You never would have had any property to mis-manage, if it had n't been for her; and see the way ye show your gratitude for it. You won't let her go into company, nor have company at home; you won't allow a hired girl in the house, but she and Maria have to do all the drudgery. You make perfect slaves of 'em. I swear, if 't wa'n't for your wife, I would n't work for you an hour longer; but she's the best woman in the world, after all you 've done to break her spirit, and I hate to leave her.'

" The old fellow squirmed, and wrenched the crowbar in the ground, then snarled back : 'Yes ! you 're waitin' for me to die; then you mean to step into my shoes.'

" ' I hope you 'll leave a decenter pair than them you 've got on, if I 'm to step into 'em,' says I.

" ' One thing about it,' says he, ' she won't have ye.'

" ' I should think,' says I, ' a woman that would marry you would have 'most anybody.'

" So we had it back and forth, till by and by he left me to throw off the rails, and went to show the boys how to build the fence.

" ' Look here,' says he ; ' jest put a thunderin' big stun to each corner ; then lay your rail on ; then drive your

pair of stakes over it like a letter X.' He drove a pair.
'Now put on your rider. There's your letter X, ridin'
one length of rails and carryin' another. That's what I
call puttin' yer alphabet to a practical use; and I say
there a'n't no sense in havin' any more edication than ye
can put to a practical use. I've larnin' enough to git
along in the world; and if my boys have as much as I've
got, they'll git along. Now work spry, for there comes
Deacon Talcott.'

"'Wal, wal!' says the Deacon, coming up, puffing with
excitement; 'what ye doin' to the old meetin'-house?'

"'Wal,' says Jedwort, driving away at his stakes, and
never looking up, 'I've been considerin' some time what I
should do with 't, and I've concluded to make a barn on 't.'

"'Make a barn! make a barn!' cries the Deacon.
'Who give ye liberty to make a barn of the house of God?'

"'Nobody; I take the liberty. Why should n't I do
what I please with my own prop'ty?'

"'Your own property, — what do ye mean? 'T a'n't
your meetin'-house.'

"'Whose is 't, if 't a'n't mine?' says Jedwort, lifting his
turtle's head from between his horizontal shoulders, and
grinning in the Deacon's face.

"'It belongs to the society,' says the Deacon.

"'But the s'ciety's pulled up stakes and gone off.'

"'It belongs to individooals of the society, — to individooals.'

"'Wal, I'm an individooal,' says Jedwort.

"'You! you never went to meetin' here a dozen times
in your life!'

"'I never did have my share of the old meetin'-house,
that's a fact,' says Jedwort; 'but I'll make it up now.'

"'But what are ye fencin' up the common for?' says
the Deacon.

" ' It 'll make a good calf-pastur'. I 've never had my share o' the vally o' that, either. I 've let my neighbors' pigs and critters run on 't long enough ; and now I 'm jest goin' to take possession o' my own.'

" ' Your own !' says the Deacon, in perfect consternation. ' You 've no deed on 't.'

" ' Wal, have you?'

" ' No — but — the society —'

" ' The s'ciety, I tell ye,' says Jedwort, holding his head up longer than I ever knew him to hold it up at a time, and grinning all the while in Talcott's face, — ' the s'ciety is split to pieces. There a'n't no s'ciety now, — any more 'n a pig 's a pig arter you 've butchered and e't it. You 've e't the pig amongst ye, and left me the pen. The s'ciety never had a deed o' this 'ere prop'ty ; and no man never had a deed o' this 'ere prop'ty. My wife's gran'daddy, when he took up the land here, was a good-natered sort of man, and he allowed a corner on 't for his neighbors to put up a temp'rary meetin'-house. That was finally used up, — the kind o' preachin' they had them days was enough to use up in a little time any house that wa'n't fire-proof ; and when that was preached to pieces, they put up another shelter in its place. This is it. And now 't the land a'n't used no more for the puppose 't was lent for, it goes back nat'rally to the estate 't was took from, and the buildin's along with it.'

" ' That 's all a sheer fabrication,' says the Deacon. ' This land was never a part of what 's now your farm, any more than it was a part of mine.'

" ' Wal,' says Jedwort, ' I look at it in my way, and you 've a perfect right to look at it in your way. But I 'm goin' to make sure o' my way, by puttin' a fence round the hull concern.'

" ' And you 're usin' some of my rails for to do it with !' says the Deacon.

" 'Can you swear 't they 're your rails ?'

" 'Yes, I can; they 're rails the freshet carried off from my farm last spring, and landed onto yourn.'

" 'So I 've heard ye say. But can you swear to the partic'lar rails ? Can you swear, for instance, 't this 'ere is your rail ? or this 'ere one ?'

" 'No; I can't swear to precisely them two, — but — '

" 'Can you swear to these two ? or to any one or two ?' says Jedwort. 'No, ye can't. Ye can swear to the lot in general, but you can't swear to any partic'lar rail, and that kind o' swearin' won't stand law, Deacon Talcott. I don't boast of bein' an edicated man, but I know suthin' o' what law is, and when I know it, I dror a line there, and I toe that line, and I make my neighbors toe that line, Deacon Talcott. Nine p'ints of the law is possession, and I 'll have possession o' this 'ere house and land by fencin' on 't in ; and though every man 't comes along should say these 'ere rails belong to them, I 'll fence it in with these 'ere very rails.'

. " Jedwort said this, wagging his obstinate old head, and grinning with his face turned up pugnaciously at the Deacon ; then went to work again as if he had settled the question, and did n't wish to discuss it any further.

" As for Talcott, he was too full of wrath and boiling indignation to answer such a speech. He knew that Jedwort had managed to get the start of him with regard to the rails, by mixing a few of his own with those he had stolen, so that nobody could tell 'em apart ; and he saw at once that the meeting-house was in danger of going the same way, just for want of an owner to swear out a clear title to the property. He did just the wisest thing when he swallowed his vexation, and hurried off to alarm the leading men of the two societies, and to consult a lawyer.

" 'He 'll stir up the old town like a bumble-bee's nest,'

says Jedwort. 'Hurry up, boys, or there'll be a buzzin' round our ears 'fore we git through!'

"'I wish ye would n't, pa!' says Dave. 'Why don't we 'tend to our own business, and be decent, like other folks? I 'm sick of this kind of life.'

"'Quit it, then,' says Jedwort.

"'Do you tell me to quit it?' says Dave, dropping the end of a rail he was handling.

"'Yes, I do; and do it dumbed quick, if ye can't show a proper respect to your father!'

"Dave turned white as a sheet, and he trembled as he answered back, 'I should be glad to show you respect, if you was a man I could feel any respect for.'

"At that, Jedwort caught hold of the iron bar that was sticking in the ground, where he had been making a hole for a stake, and pulled away at it. 'I 'll make a stake-hole in you!' says he. 'It 's enough to have a sassy hired man round, without bein' jawed by one's own children!'

"Dave was out of reach by the time the bar came out of the ground.

"'Come here, you villain!' says the old man.

"'I 'd rather be excused,' says Dave, backing off. 'I don't want any stake-holes made in me to-day. You told me to quit, and I 'm going to. You may steal your own meeting-houses in future; I won't help.'

"There was a short race. Dave's young legs proved altogether too smart for the old waddler's, and he got off. Then Jedwort, coming back, wheezing and sweating, with his iron bar, turned savagely on me.

"'I 've a good notion to tell you to go too!'

"'Very well, why don't ye?' says I. 'I 'm ready.'

"'There 's no livin' with ye, ye 're gittin' so dumbed sassy! What I keep ye for is a mystery to me.'

"'No, it a'n't; you keep me because you can't get an-

other man to fill my place.   You put up with my sass for
the money I bring ye in.'

"'Hold your yawp,' says he, 'and go and git another
load of rails.   If ye see Dave, tell him to come back to
work.'

"I did see Dave, but, instead of telling him to go back,
I advised him to put out from the old home and get his
living somewhere else.   His mother and Maria agreed with
me; and when the old man came home that night, Dave
was gone.

"When I got back with my second load, I found the
neighbors assembling to witness the stealing of the old
meeting-house, and Jedwort was answering their remon-
strances.

"'A meetin'-house is a respectable kind o' prop'ty to
have round,' says he.   'The steeple 'll make a good show
behind my house.   When folks ride by, they 'll stop and
look, and say, "There 's a man keeps a private meetin'-
house of his own."   I can have preachin' in 't, too, if I
want.   I 'm able to hire a preacher of my own, or I can
preach myself and save the expense.'

"Of course, neither sarcasm nor argument could have
any effect on such a man.   As the neighbors were going
away, Jedwort shouted after 'em: 'Call agin.   Glad to see
ye.   There 'll be more sport in a few days, when I take the
dumbed thing away.'   (The dumbed thing was the meeting-house.)   'I invite ye all to see the show.   Free gratis.
It 'll be good as a circus, and a 'tarnal sight cheaper.   The
women can bring their knittin', and the gals their ever-
lastin' tattin'.   As it 'll be a pious kind o' show, bein' it 's
a meetin'-house, guess I 'll have notices gi'n out from the
pulpits the Sunday afore.'

"The common was fenced in by sundown; and the next
day Jedwort had over a house-mover from the North Vil-

lage to look and see what could be done with the building.
'Can ye snake it over, and drop it back of my house?'
says he.

"'It'll be a hard job,' says old Bob, 'without you tear
down the steeple fust.'

"But Jedwort said, 'What's a meetin'-house 'thout a
steeple? I've got my heart kind o' set on that steeple,
and I'm bound to go the hull hog on this 'ere concern,
now I've begun.'

"'I vow,' says Bob, examining the timbers, 'I won't
warrant but what the old thing 'll all tumble down.'

"'I'll resk it.'

"'Yes; but who'll resk the lives of me and my men?'

"'O, you'll see if it's re'ly goin' to tumble, and look
out. I'll engage 't me and my boys 'll do the most dangerous part of the work. Dumbed if I would n't agree to
ride in the steeple and ring the bell, if there was one.'

"I've never heard that the promised notices were read
from the pulpits; but it was n't many days before Bob
came over again, bringing with him this time his screws
and ropes and rollers, his men and timbers, horse and cap-
stan; and at last the old house might have been seen on
its travels.

"It was an exciting time all around. The societies
found that Jedwort's fence gave him the first claim to
house and land, unless a regular siege of the law was gone
through to beat him off, — and then it might turn out
that he would beat them. Some said fight him; some
said let him be, — the thing a'n't worth going to law for;
and so, as the leading men could n't agree as to what
should be done, nothing was done. That was just what
Jedwort had expected, and he laughed in his sleeve while
Bob and his boys screwed up the old meeting-house, and
got their beams under it, and set it on rollers, and slued it

around, and slid it on the timbers laid for it across into
Jedwort's field, steeple foremost, like a locomotive on a
track.

"It was a trying time for the women-folks at home.
Maria had declared that, if her father did persist in stealing the meeting-house, she would not stay a single day
after it, but would follow Dave.

"That touched me pretty close, for, to tell the truth, it
was rather more Maria than her mother that kept me at
work for the old man. 'If you go,' says I, 'then there is
no object for me to stay; I shall go too.'

"'That's what I supposed,' says she; 'for there's no
reason in the world why you should stay. But then Dan
will go; and who'll be left to take sides with mother?
That's what troubles me. O, if she could only go too!
But she won't; and she couldn't if she would, with the
other children depending on her. Dear, dear! what shall
we do?'

"The poor girl put her head on my shoulder, and cried;
and if I should own up to the truth, I suppose I cried a
little too. For where's the man that can hold a sweet
woman's head on his shoulder, while she sobs out her
trouble, and he has n't any power to help her — who, I
say, can do any less, under such circumstances, than drop
a tear or two for company?

"'Never mind; don't hurry,' says Mrs. Jedwort. 'Be
patient, and wait awhile, and it'll all turn out right, I'm
sure.'

"'Yes, you always say, "Be patient, and wait!"' says
Maria, brushing back her hair. 'But, for my part, I'm
tired of waiting, and my patience has given out long ago.
We can't always live in this way, and we may as well make
a change now as ever. But I can't bear the thought of
going and leaving you.'

"Here the two younger girls came in; and, seeing that crying was the order of the day, they began to cry; and when they heard Maria talk of going, they declared they would go; and even little Willie, the four-year-old, began to howl.

" 'There, there! Maria! Lottie! Susie!' said Mrs. Jedwort, in her calm way; 'Willie, hush up! I don't know what we are to do; but I feel that something is going to happen that will show us the right way, and we are to wait. Now go and wash the dishes, and set the cheese.'

"That was just after breakfast, the second day of the moving; and sure enough, something like what she prophesied did happen before another sun.

"The old frame held together pretty well till along toward night, when the steeple showed signs of seceding. 'There she goes! She's falling now!' sung out the boys, who had been hanging around all day in hopes of seeing the thing tumble.

"The house was then within a few rods of where Jedwort wanted it; but Bob stopped right there, and said it was n't safe to haul it another inch. 'That steeple 's bound to come down, if we do,' says he.

" 'Not by a dumbed sight, it a'n't,' says Jedwort. 'Them cracks a'n't nothin'; the j'ints is all firm yit.' He wanted Bob to go up and examine; but Bob shook his head, — the concern looked too shaky. Then he told me to go up; but I said I had n't lived quite long enough, and had a little rather be smoking my pipe on *terra firma*. Then the boys began to hoot. 'Dumbed if ye a'n't all a set of cowards,' says he. 'I 'll go up myself.'

"We waited outside while he climbed up inside. The boys jumped on the ground to jar the steeple, and make it fall. One of them blew a horn, — as he said, to bring down the old Jericho, — and another thought he 'd help

things along by starting up the horse, and giving the building a little wrench. But Bob put a stop to that; and
finally out came a head from the belfry window. It was
Jedwort, who shouted down to us: 'There a'n't a j'int or
brace gin out. Start the hoss, and I'll ride. Pass me up
that 'ere horn, and —'

"Just then there came a cracking and loosening of timbers; and we that stood nearest had only time to jump
out of the way, when down came the steeple crashing to
the ground, with Jedwort in it."

"I hope it killed the cuss," said one of the village story-
tellers.

"Worse than that," replied my friend; "it just cracked
his skull, — not enough to put an end to his miserable life,
but only to take away what little sense he had. We got
the doctors to him, and they patched up his broken head;
and, by George, it made me mad to see the fuss the women-folks made over him. It would have been my way to
let him die; but they were as anxious and attentive to
him as if he had been the kindest husband and most in-
dulgent father that ever lived; for that's women's style:
they're unreasoning creatures.

"Along towards morning, we persuaded Mrs. Jedwort,
who had been up all night, to lie down a spell and catch
a little rest, while Maria and I sat up and watched with
the old man. All was still except our whispers and his
heavy breathing; there was a lamp burning in the next
room; when all of a sudden a light shone into the win-
dows, and about the same time we heard a roaring and
crackling sound. We looked out, and saw the night all
lighted up, as if by some great fire. As it appeared to be
on the other side of the house, we ran to the door, and
there what did we see but the old meeting-house all in
flames. Some fellows had set fire to it to spite Jedwort.

It must have been burning some time inside ; for when we looked out the flames had burst through the roof.

"As the night was perfectly still, except a light wind blowing away from the other buildings on the place, we raised no alarm, but just stood in the door and saw it burn. And a glad sight it was to us, you may be sure. I just held Maria close to my side, and told her that all was well, — it was the best thing that could happen. 'O yes,' says she, 'it seems to me as though a kind Providence was burning up his sin and shame out of our sight.'

"I had never yet said anything to her about marriage, — for the time to come at that had never seemed to arrive ; but there 's nothing like a little excitement to bring things to a focus. You 've seen water in a tumbler just at the freezing-point, but not exactly able to make up its mind to freeze, when a little jar will set the crystals forming, and in a minute what was liquid is ice. It was the shock of events that night that touched my life into crystals, — not of ice, gentlemen, by any manner of means.

"After the fire had got along so far that the meeting-house was a gone case, an alarm was given, probably by the very fellows that set it, and a hundred people were on the spot before the thing had done burning.

" Of course these circumstances put an end to the breaking up of the family. Dave was sent for, and came home. Then, as soon as we saw that the old man's brain was injured so that he was n't likely to recover his mind, the boys and I went to work and put that farm through a course of improvement it would have done your eyes good to see. The children were sent to school, and Mrs. Jedwort had all the money she wanted now to clothe them, and to provide the house with comforts, without stealing her own butter. Jedwort was a burden ; but, in spite of him, that was just about the happiest family, for the next four years, that ever lived on this planet.

" Jedwort soon got his bodily health, but I don't think he knew one of us again after his hurt. As near as I could get at his state of mind, he thought he had been changed into some sort of animal. He seemed inclined to take me for a master, and for four years he followed me around like a dog. During that time he never spoke, but only whined and growled. When I said, ' Lie down,' he'd lie down ; and when I whistled he'd come.

" I used sometimes to make him work ; and certain simple things he would do very well, as long as I was by. One day I had a jag of hay to get in ; and, as the boys were away, I thought I'd have him load it. I pitched it on to the wagon about where it ought to lie, and looked to him only to pack it down. There turned out to be a bigger load than I had expected, and the higher it got, the worse the shape of it, till finally, as I was starting it towards the barn, off it rolled, and the old man with it, head foremost.

" He struck a stone heap, and for a moment I thought he was killed. But he jumped up and spoke for the first time. ' *I'll blow it*,' says he, finishing the sentence he had begun four years before, when he called for the horn to be passed up to him.

" I could n't have been much more astonished if one of the horses had spoken. But I saw at once that there was an expression in Jedwort's face that had n't been there since his tumble in the belfry ; and I knew that, as his wits had been knocked out of him by one blow on the head, so another blow had knocked 'em in again.

" ' Where's Bob ?' says he, looking all around.

" ' Bob ?' says I, not thinking at first who he meant. ' O, Bob is dead, — he has been dead these three years.'

" Without noticing my reply, he exclaimed : ' Where did all that hay come from ? Where's the old meetin'-house ?'

"'Don't you know?' says I. 'Some rogues set fire to it the night after you got hurt, and burnt it up.'

"He seemed then just beginning to realize that something extraordinary had happened.

"'Stark,' says he, 'what's the matter with ye? You're changed.'

"'Yes,' says I, 'I wear my beard now, and I've grown older!'

"'Dumbed if 't a'n't odd!' says he. 'Stark, what in thunder's the matter with *me?*'

"'You've had meeting-house on the brain for the past four years,' says I; 'that's what's the matter.'

"It was some time before I could make him understand that he had been out of his head, and that so long a time had been a blank to him.

"Then he said, 'Is this my farm?'

"'Don't you know it?' says I.

"'It looks more slicked up than ever it used to,' says he.

"'Yes,' says I; 'and you'll find everything else on the place slicked up in about the same way.'

"'Where's Dave?' says he.

"'Dave has gone to town to see about selling the wool.'

"'Where's Dan?'

"'Dan's in college. He takes a great notion to medicine; and we're going to make a doctor of him.'

"'Whose house is that?' says he, as I was taking him home.

"'No wonder you don't know it,' says I. 'It has been painted, and shingled, and had new blinds put on; the gates and fences are all in prime condition; and that's a new barn we put up a couple of years ago.'

"'Where does the money come from, to make all these improvements?'

"'It comes off the place,' says I. 'We have n't run in

debt the first cent for anything, but we 've made the farm more profitable than it ever was before.'

" ' That *my* house ? ' he repeated wonderingly, as we approached it. ' What sound is that ? '

" ' That 's Lottie practising her lesson on the piano.'

" ' A pianer in my house ? ' he muttered. ' I can't stand that ! ' He listened. ' It sounds pooty, though ! '

" ' Yes, it does sound pretty, and I guess you 'll like it. How does the place suit you ? '

" ' It *looks* pooty.'· He started. ' What young lady is that ? '

" It was Lottie, who had left her music, and stood by the window.

" ' My dahter ! ye don't say ! Dumbed if she a'n't a mighty nice gal.'

" ' Yes,' says I ; ' she takes after her mother.'

" Just then Susie, who heard talking, ran to the door.

" ' Who 's that agin ? ' says Jedwort.

" I told him.

" ' Wal, *she* 's a mighty nice-lookin' gal ! '

" ' Yes,' says I, ' *she* takes after her mother.'

" Little Willie, now eight years old, came out of the wood-shed with a bow-and-arrow in his hand, and stared like an owl, hearing his father talk.

" ' What boy is that ? ' says Jedwort. And when I told him, he muttered, ' He 's an ugly-looking brat ! '

" ' He 's more like his father,' says I.

" The truth is, Willie was such a fine boy the old man was afraid to praise him, for fear I 'd say of him, as I 'd said of the girls, that he favored his mother.

" Susie ran back and gave the alarm ; and then out came mother, and Maria with her baby in her arms, — for I forgot to tell you that we had been married now nigh on to two years.

" Well, the women-folks were as much astonished as I had
been when Jedwort first spoke, and a good deal more delighted. They drew him into the house; and I am bound
to say he behaved remarkably well. He kept looking at
his wife, and his children, and his grandchild, and the new
paper on the walls, and the new furniture, and now and then
asking a question or making a remark.

" ' It all comes back to me now,' says he at last. ' I
thought I was living in the moon, with a superior race of
human bein's; and this is the place, and you are the
people.'

" It was n't more than a couple of days before he began
to pry around, and find fault, and grumble at the expense;
and I saw there was danger of things relapsing into something like their former condition. So I took him one side,
and talked to him.

" ' Jedwort,' says I, ' you 're like a man raised from the
grave. You was the same as buried to your neighbors,
and now they come and look at you as they would at a
dead man come to life. To you, it 's like coming into a new
world; and I 'll leave it to you now, if you don't rather
like the change from the old state of things to what you
see around you to-day. You 've seen how the family af-
fairs go on, — how pleasant everything is, and how we all
enjoy ourselves. You hear the piano, and like it; you see
your children sought after and respected, — your wife in
finer health and spirits than you 've ever known her since
the day she was married; you see industry and neatness
everywhere on the premises; and you 're a beast if you
don't like all that. In short, you see that our management
is a great deal better than yours; and that we beat you,
even in the matter of economy. Now, what I want to know
is this: whether you think you 'd like to fall into our way
of living, or return like a hog to your wallow.'

" ' I don't say but what I like your way of livin' very well,' he grumbled.

" ' Then,' says I, ' you must just let us go ahead, as we have been going ahead. Now 's the time for you to turn about and be a respectable man, like your neighbors. Just own up, and say you 've not only been out of your head the past four years, but that you 've been more or less out of your head the last four-and-twenty years. But say you 're in your right mind now, and prove it by acting like a man in his right mind. Do that, and I 'm with you ; we 're all with you. But go back to your old dirty ways, and you go alone. Now I sha' n't let you off till you tell me what you mean to do.'

" He hesitated some time, then said, ' Maybe you 're about right, Stark ; you and Dave and the old woman seem to be doin' pooty well, and I guess I 'll let you go on.' "

Here my friend paused, as if his story was done ; when one of the villagers asked, " About the land where the old meetin'-house stood, — what ever was done with that ? "

" That was appropriated for a new school-house ; and there my little shavers go to school."

" And old Jedwort, is he alive yet ? "

" Both Jedwort and his wife have gone to that country where meanness and dishonesty have a mighty poor chance, — where the only investments worth much are those recorded in the Book of Life. Mrs. Jedwort was rich in that kind of stock ; and Jedwort's account, I guess, will compare favorably with that of some respectable people, such as we all know. I tell ye, my friends," continued my fellow-traveller, " there 's many a man, both in the higher and lower ranks of life, that 't would do a deal of good, say nothing of the mercy 't would be to their fam-

ilies, just to knock 'em on the head, and make Nebuchad-
nezzars of 'em, — then, after they 'd been turned out to grass
a few years, let 'em come back again, and see how happy
folks have been, and how well they have got along without 'em.

"I carry on the old place now," he added. "The younger girls are married off; Dan's a doctor in the North
Village; and as for Dave, he and I have struck ile. I 'm
going out to look at our property now."

PREACHING FOR SELWYN.

I.

MR. JERVEY'S PART OF THE STORY.

"I AM one of the keepers at the Asylum, you know.

"The Asylum stands on a hill; not much of a hill, either, but just a pretty elevation of ground, with a noble lawn sloping down to the river-bank, from which it is separated by a high board fence. None of your commonplace fences, understand, such as seem often to have no other use than just to spoil a landscape. You would say that, as a general thing, a fence like that about an estate must be designed for keeping people out. This, though, was meant to keep people in. The people, in our case, are the inmates of the Asylum." And Mr. Jervey touched his forehead significantly.

"There was a wicket in the fence, that opened into a boat-house, that opened at the other end on to the water. There the doctor kept his boat, in which we gave the patients many a fine row and sail. For he was one of your right-down sensible, kind-hearted doctors; none of your — Well, I won't draw comparisons, for fear I may be considered wanting in respect toward his very worthy successor.

"He — I mean the old doctor — believed in the wholesome influence of kindness and change of scene and mild recreation on his patients. So he was always thinking of

little things that would cheer and amuse them. Saturday
nights, and occasionally at other times, the boat-house was
turned into a bathing-house for a certain class of patients.
Of course it was only a certain class that could be trusted
either to go on or into the water. 'It always has
a good effect to trust those that can be trusted,' says
the doctor. Then, you know, the boat and the bath, and
all such things, worked well, held out as rewards for
good behavior.

"One Sunday morning, a new patient we had just got in
complained to me that he had been promised a swim in
the river, but that nothing had been said to him when the
others went in the night before. He was so very anxious
for his bath that morning, that I thought 't would do no
harm to lay his case before the doctor.

"'What do you think of him, Jervey?' says the doctor.

"'Very quiet, very gentlemanly,' says I.

"'Bring him to me,' says the doctor.

"So I went and brought Mr. Hillbright, — for that was
the man's name, — and introduced him with the little for-
mality usually pleasing to that kind of people.

"'Mr. Hillbright, Doctor,' says I.

"'Ah! good morning, Mr. Hillbright,' says the doctor.
'How are you this morning?'

"'Very well indeed, Doctor, I thank you kindly,' says
the patient. He was a man of about five-and-forty, well
dressed, and very gentlemanly, as I have said; belonged to
a good family; rather fleshy; a little bald on the top of
his head; but with nothing very peculiar in his appearance
except a quick way of speaking, and a quick way of dropping his eyes before you every now and then. 'Very well
indeed, Doctor,' says he; 'only the sins of the world weigh
upon me very heavily, as you are aware.' And in the most
solemn manner he bowed that bald-topped head of his until

the doctor, where he sat, could have reached up and written his name on it.

"'O yes, I know,' says the doctor. 'They weigh upon me too. But we shall get rid of the burden in good time, — all in good time, Mr. Hillbright.'

"That was the doctor's style of managing patients of this sort. It did no good to contradict them, he said, but if you could convince one that his case was n't peculiar, that others had had similar troubles and been cured of 'em, that was the first step toward bringing him around to his right senses. So, if one complained that he had a devil, the doctor would very likely relate to him in confidence how he had had a much bigger devil, and how he had got rid of him. 'I 'm in hell! I 'm in hell, Doctor!' says a woman to him. 'I don't doubt it; a great many people are,' says the doctor; 'I have been there myself.' And that would usually throw cold water on the fire sooner than anything.

" Hillbright was quite taken aback by the doctor's candid admission and expression of sympathy ; for I suppose he had never been treated with anything but contradiction and argument till he came to us. But he rallied in a minute and said, glib as a parrot, 'I have taken the sins of the world,' says he, 'and I must bear them till I am permited to preach and convert the world. Meanwhile the world hates me, and all I can do for my relief is to go down into the river and be baptized. I need n't explain to a philosopher like you,' says he, bowing again to the doctor, 'that some of the sins will wash off.'

"The doctor approved of the idea, and said : 'Jervey,' says he, 'always have a bath-tub at Mr. Hillbright's disposal.'

"'A bath-tub?' says Hillbright, with a sort of sorrowful

amazement ; 'the sins of the world in a bath-tub? The
ocean would n't hold them !'

" 'Jervey,' says the doctor, 'give the sins of the world
a good plunge into the river this morning.'

" So I took the key of the boat-house and went down
with my man to the shore.

" He had n't been long in the water when he made an
awful discovery. The sins would n't wash off ! He must
have soap, and there was only one sort that would serve
his purpose. He said I would find a cake of it on the little table in his room, and begged me to go and get it.

" I did n't like to lose sight of him ; but the doctor had
told me always to humor his patients in trifling matters
which they considered important. ' For even if we can't
cure 'em,' says he, 'we can at least make 'em comfortable' ;
and going for a cake of soap was so little trouble, and besides, as I said, Hillbright was such a quiet, respectable,
gentlemanly person, I thought him safe, especially if I
kept possession of his clothes. They were in the boat-
house locker, where I always kept the clothes of the bath-
ers ; so I just turned the key on 'em and went for the
soap, leaving Mr. Hillbright to give the sins of the world a
good soaking till I came back.

" I had a pretty good hunt, finding nothing on his table
but a small pocket Bible, about the size and shape of the
thing I expected to find, but not the thing itself. It occurred to me in a minute, though, that this was really
what the man wanted ; for where else was the kind of
soap that would wash away the sins of the world ? I
grinned a little at my own previous simplicity, but determined that nobody else should have a chance to grin at
it, least of all my man in the water ; so I took the Bible,
and says I to myself, ' I 'll hand it to him as if it was
actually a cake of soap, and I had understood his subtle

meaning from the first; and then see what he will do with it.'

"I unlocked the little door in the fence, and entered the boat-house, and was immediately struck by an odd look it had, as if something strange had taken place in my absence. The boat — yes, that was it — the boat was gone! I ran along the narrow side of the platform to the door opening on the river, and looked out, — about as anxiously as I ever looked out of a door in my life : there was the river, running smoothly, and looking as innocent of the sins of the world, and the morning was looking as still and lovely, as any river or any Sunday morning that ever you saw. But there was no boat and no Hillbright to be seen ; boat, Hillbright, sins of the world, all had disappeared together.

"I ran back to the locker, and found the man's clothes all right. My respectable, gentlemanly patient had launched himself into society in a surprising state of nature, — a thing I had n't for a moment believed him capable of doing, he was always so very distant, I may say formal, in his deportment. What with his mystical cake of soap, and his running away as soon as I was out of sight, I own he had fooled me most completely.

"Now, I lay it down as a general principle that nobody likes to be taken in, even by a man in his senses. Still less do you fancy that sort of humiliation from a man out of his senses. Then put the case of a person in my position, — a keeper, supposed to have more experience and wit in dealing with the insane than you outsiders can have, — and you perceive how very crushing a circumstance it must have been to me.

"I ran like a deer down the river-bank, till I came to the bend, around which I felt sure of getting a sight of the boat. I was right there ; I found the boat, but it was

adrift, and going down with the current, without anybody
aboard. There was no Hillbright to be seen, afloat or
ashore, and it was n't possible to tell which way he had
gone, for the high fence had concealed his movements, and
then the river-banks below were fringed with trees and
bushes on both sides. So all I could do was to hurry back
to the house, give the alarm, and get all hands out on the
hunt for him, that fine Sunday morning."

Thus far our friend Jervey.

II.

PARSON DODD AND THE BAY MARE.

PARSON DODD was to be that day a partner in a triangu-
lar exchange. That is, Dodd was to preach for Selwyn,
Selwyn was to preach for Burdick, and Burdick was to
preach for Dodd.

From Dodd's parish at Coldwater to Selwyn's at Longtrot was a distance of some fourteen miles. Just a nice
little Sunday morning's drive in fine weather ; and one to
which Dodd looked forward with interest, for two or three
reasons.

To begin with, Dodd was a bachelor of full five-and-
forty. He had always intended to marry, but being one
of your procrastinating gentlemen, who make it a rule to
put off until to-morrow whatever they are not absolutely
compelled to do to-day, he had, with other things, put off
matrimony. He had even paid somewhat marked and
prolonged attentions — at different periods, of course — to
three or four ladies, each of whom had in turn been
snatched up by a more enterprising suitor, while he was

slowly making up his mind on the subject of a proposal. Very much as if he had been contemplating a fair morsel on his fork, expecting in due time to swallow it, but in no haste to do so, when some puppy had rushed in and swallowed it for him, with a celerity that quite took the good man's breath away.

Not that Garcey was a puppy, by any means. He was a brother clergyman, and Selwyn's predecessor at Longtrot; and there was a time when he liked wonderfully well to come over and preach for Dodd. And that is the way he became connected with the romance of Dodd's life.

To the last of the estimable ladies alluded to — namely, Miss Melissa Wortleby, of his parish — Dodd did actually propose matrimony, after taking about five years to think of it. But Miss Wortleby was then aghast at an offer which would have made her the happiest of women three days ago.

"Dear me, Mr. Dodd!" said she. "Why did n't you ever tell me, if you had such a thing in your mind?"

The parson stammered out that a serious step of that nature was not to be taken in haste. "There 's always time enough, you are aware, Miss Wortleby."

"Yes," said poor Miss Wortleby, with a look of distress; "but Mr. Garcey — he — he proposed to me last Sunday, and I —"

"You accepted him?" said Parson Dodd, turning pale at this unexpected stroke.

Miss Wortleby's tears were a sufficient confession.

"The traitor!" said Parson Dodd. "He took advantage of our exchange to offer himself to you. He has taken advantage of many another exchange, I suppose, to come over and cultivate your acquaintance. Always teasing me for an exchange — the vil —"

"No, no, dear Mr. Dodd!" pleaded Melissa Wortleby,

clasping his hands. "He is no traitor and no villain. He had no idea, any more than I had, that you — "

"To be sure," said Parson Dodd, resuming that serene behavior and those just sentiments which were habitual with him. "I have nobody to blame but myself, dear Miss Wortleby."

Dodd must have seen that he was really the young lady's choice, and that it would have been no very difficult task to prevail upon her to cancel her hasty engagement with Garcey. But we must do him the justice to say that if he was given to procrastination in matters of right, he was still more slow to decide upon any course of doubtful morality. So he stepped gracefully aside, and gave the pair to each other in a very literal sense, himself performing the wedding ceremony.

Garcey was settled, as I said, in what was now Selwyn's parish; there he lived with his gentle Melissa, preached two or three times a week (exchanging very rarely with Dodd in those days, however), and laid the foundations of a wide reputation and a large family. Then he died, leaving to his afflicted widow a barrel of sermons and six children.

Melissa still lived at the parsonage over at Longtrot, and boarded Selwyn, the young theological sprig, lately slipped from the academical tree and planted in that parish in the hope that he might take root there. It was even whispered that he was likely to take root there in a double sense, succeeding the lamented Garcey not only in the pulpit, but also in Mrs. Garcey's affections. But of course there was no truth in that suspicion. Parson Dodd must have known there was no truth in it, for he would have been the last man to serve another as poor Garcey had served him. And somehow Dodd liked to preach for Selwyn.

To be quite frank about the matter, Parson Dodd had lately awakened one morning and discovered to his surprise the marks of age creeping over him. His crown was getting bald, his waistcoat round, his hair (what there was of it) silvery (but he wore a wig), his frontal ivory golden. Until yesterday he had said of growing old, as of everything else, "Time enough for that." But however man may procrastinate, the old fellow with the scythe and the forelock is always about his work; and here was Dodd's field of life more than half mown before he knew it. "Only a little patch of withered herbage left!" thought he with consternation.

Of course no *young* lady would think of having him now. He might have deemed his case hopeless, but there was the mother of Garcey's innocents! I'll not say that these living monuments to the memory of his late friend were not just a little dampening to the ardor of his reviving attachment. Of all the ready-made articles with which the world abounds, one of the least desirable is a ready-made family. To bear with easy grace a weighty domestic responsibility (and a wife and six may be considered such), one should begin with it at the beginning, like the man in the fable, who, by shouldering the calf daily, came at last to carry the ox. But to commence married life where another man has left off, that requires courage. But Dodd was a man of courage; one of those who, irresolute and dilatory in ordinary matters, show unexpected pluck in the face of formidable undertakings. He had thought of all these things. And, as I have said, he liked to preach for Selwyn.

Usually, when he had that privilege, he drove over to Longtrot early in the morning, put up his horse at the parsonage, and had a good hour with the relict of the lamented Garcey before the ringing of the second bell. An hour spent probably in Scriptural readings and conversations, or perhaps in drilling the little Garceys in their Sunday-school lessons. Whatever the pious task, his heart was evidently in it; for it was always noticeable afterward when he walked to church with the widow and her little tribe, leading the youngest between them, that his kind face beamed with peculiar satisfaction.

But, as I have hinted, there was other cause for the interest with which Parson Dodd looked forward to this particular Sunday morning's ride. Shall I confess it? The worthy man, having no family, was a lover of animals, especially of horses, — more especially of fine horses. He had lately exchanged nags (an act which in a layman is termed "swapping") and got a bay mare; to his experienced eye a very superior beast to the one he put away. He had as yet had no opportunity to try her paces for more than a short spirt; but he liked the way she carried her hoofs, and he believed her to be "sound and true." He had her of a townsman, — Colonel Jakes, — who, though something of a jockey, was never known actually to lie about a horse; and Colonel Jakes had said, as he turned the quid in his cheek, and squinted with a professional air across the mare's fetlocks, and looked candid as a summer's day, "There's lots of travel in that beast, Parson. You see how she goes off; and it's my experience she's poorest at the start. Yes, Parson, I give ye my word, you'll find that creatur's generally poorest at the start. You'll say so when you've drove her a little."

It was a lovely morning, and the heart of Parson Dodd was happy in his breast, when he set off, at half past seven o'clock, alone in his buggy, driving the bay mare, to go over and preach for Selwyn.

He was very carefully dressed in his dark brown wig, his suit of handsome blue-black cloth, and ruffled shirt-

bosom of snowy whiteness, which distinguished him among
clergymen far and near. "Let me see that coat and that
shirt-bosom anywhere, and I should know it was you," said
Mrs. Bean, with just pride in her washing and in her minister, that very morning. "But," her eye resting with
some surprise on his neckcloth, "where *did* you git that
imbroidered new white neck-handkerchief?"

"A gift, — a gift from a lady," replied Parson Dodd,
evasively.

He was not quite prepared to inform her that his appearance in it foreboded a change in her housekeeping.
But so it was. In the note that came with it a few days
before, Melissa had written with a trembling hand : "I embroidered it for my dear husband. Will you accept and
wear it?" Of course, these simple, pathetic words were
not in any way designed as a nudge to Dodd's well-known
procrastinating disposition. Yet he could not but feel that
putting on the neckcloth that morning was as good as
tying the matrimonial halter under his chin.

"Wal, I don't care, it 's perty anyhow!" said Mrs. Bean.

So Parson Dodd started off, wearing the fatal neckcloth,
and driving the bay mare. Her coat was glossy as silk ;
the air was exhilarating ; the birds sang sweetly ; she
stepped off beautifully. He knew Melissa would be expecting him, and he was happy.

"But hold on!" said he, pulling the rein all at once.
"Bless me, my sermon!" The bay mare and the embroidered neckcloth had quite put that out of his head.
"If I had really gone without it, I should have had to
overhaul some of poor Garcey's," thought he, as he wheeled
about.

He wheeled again as he drove up to the gate, and called
to Mrs. Bean to go into his study and hand him down his
sermon-case, which she would find lying on his desk. As

she reached it to him over the gate, he remarked, "You have n't seen how she moves off."

"No, I ha'n't," said Mrs. Bean.

Parson Dodd tightened the reins, — those electric conductors through which every born driver knows how to send magnetic intelligence, the soul of the man at one end inspiring the soul of the horse at the other. And Parson Dodd clucked lightly. But Queen Bess (that was the name of her) did not move. A louder cluck, and a closer tension of the quivering ribbons. Queen Bess merely laid her ears back, curled down her tail as if she expected a blow, and — Dodd could see by the sparkling black eye turned back at him — looked vicious.

"Go 'long !" said Parson Dodd, showing the whip.

Queen Bess quietly braced herself. She was evidently used to this sort of thing, and prepared for a struggle. Parson Dodd saw the situation at a glance, remembered the jockey's declaration that she was "generally poorest at the start," and blushed to the apex of his bald crown.

"What is the matter with him?" cried sympathetic Mrs. Bean.

"*Him*'s balky, that's what's the matter," replied the irritated parson. "Go 'long, Bess, I tell you !" And he touched her shoulder with the whip.

The touch was followed by a sharp cut ; but Bess only cringed her tail more closely, and looked wickeder than ever. Then he tried coaxing. All to no purpose. It was a dead balk.

Notwithstanding his burning shame at having been shaved by a layman who "paltered with him in a double sense," and his wrath at the perverse brute, and his irritation at Mrs. Bean, who always *would* call a mare a *him*, Parson Dodd controlled his temper, and begged the lady's pardon, but told her she had better go into the house, for it might be her presence that put the devil into the brute (she declares that he said "devil"), then got out of the buggy, went to the animal's head, stroked her, patted her, spoke gently to her, and led her out into the street.

Then he once more got up into his seat. But Queen Bess saw through the transparent artifice; she had taken serious offence at the indecision shown at starting, and now she refused to start at all without leading. So Parson Dodd got out again, gave her another start with his hand on the bridle, then sprang back into the buggy, at the risk of his limbs, while she was going. "I wonder if I shall have to start in this way when I leave Melissa's?" thought he, and wondered what people would say to see *him* with a balky horse !

He let her go her own gait for a mile or two, then, by way of experiment, stopped her, and started her again. She seemed to have got over her miff by this time, for she went off readily at a word. Having repeated this experiment two or three times with encouraging success, (as if the cunning creature did n't know perfectly well what he was up to !) Parson Dodd began to think he had n't made such a fatally bad bargain after all. "With careful management, I can cure her of that trick," thought he.

When he had made about ten miles of the journey, he came to a stream where it was his custom always to "stop and water" when going over to preach for Selwyn. There was then an easy trot of four miles beyond, which he thought well for a horse after drinking ; and, besides, he considered a little soaking good for his wheels in dry weather.

Parson Dodd got out, let down the mare's check-rein, got into the buggy again, and, turning aside from the bridge, drove down into the water, purposing to drive through it and up the opposite bank, country fashion.

In mid-channel, he let Queen Bess stop and drink. She

seemed pretty thirsty, and the cautious parson, to keep her
from drinking too fast and too much, found it necessary to
pull her head up now and then. This, I suppose, vexed
her; for she was a testy creature, and could not bear to
be trifled with. At last she would not put down her head,
and, when requested to start, she would not start. In
short, Queen Bess had balked again, this time in the middle of the stream.

Parson Dodd's lips tightened across his teeth, and his
knuckles grew white about his whip-handle. But the crin-
ging tail and the leering eye told him that he might spare his
blows. Madam had fully made up her mind not to budge.

The parson stood up and reconnoitred. The stream was
thigh-deep, and it was a couple of rods to either shore.
The bridge was just out of jumping distance. There was
no help within call. Parson Dodd looked at the water,
then at his neatly fitting polished boots, ruffled shirt-bosom,
and blue-black suit, grinned, and sat down again.

"Queen Bess," said he, "you think you 've got me now.
It does look so. How long do you intend to keep me here?
Take your own time, madam! But mind, you make up
for this delay when you do start."

It was difficult, however, for a person of even so equita-
ble a temper as his own to possess his soul in patience very
long under the circumstances. Suppose Queen Bess should
conclude not to start at all that forenoon? What would
Melissa think? And who would preach for Selwyn?

There was another consideration. Queen Bess had had
her fill of cold water when she was warm, — a dangerous
thing for a horse that has been driven, and that is not kept
in exercise afterward. Before many minutes, Dodd had no
doubt she would be fatally foundered; though he did not
know but the cold water about her feet might do something toward keeping the fever from settling in them.

"This, then, is the creatur' that's usually poorest at starting! I should say so!" thought he. "I wish Colonel Jakes was lashed to her back, like another Mazeppa, and that I had the starting of her then; I'd be willing to sacrifice the mare. Come, come, Bess! good Queen Bess! Will you go 'long?"

She would not, of course.

Parson Dodd looked wistfully at both banks again, and at the inaccessible bridge, and at the hub-deep water, and said, grimly, after a moment's profound meditation, — "There's only one way; I must get out and lead her!"

It is said that the brains of drowning men are lighted at the supreme moment by a thousand vivid reflections. Parson Dodd experienced something of this phenomenon, even before he got into the water. He saw himself preaching for Selwyn in unpresentable, drenched garments, — he, the well-dressed, immaculate bachelor parson; or begging a change of the widow, and exciting great scandal in the congregation by entering the pulpit in a well-known suit of Garcey's, ("'T will be said I might at least have let his clothes alone until after I had married into them!") or waiting to be found where he was, at the mercy of a vicious mare, by the first church-going teams that came that way. Would he ever take pride in driving a neat nag, or care to preach for Selwyn, after either of these contingencies?

"I'll pull off my boots anyway; yes, and my coat; there's no use of wetting that." He stood up on his buggy-seat and looked anxiously both up and down the road, and, seeing no one, said, "I may as well save my pantaloons." Then why not his linen and underclothes? "The bath won't hurt me. Why didn't I think of this before?" said he, pulling up the buggy-top for a screen.

He began with his embroidered white neckcloth, which

he took off and placed in his hat, along with his watch, and pocket-book, and sermon, saying, at the same time, "Some leisure day, Queen Bess, you and I are going to have a settlement. Lucky for you this is n't a very favorable time for it. I 'll break your temper, or I 'll break your neck ! "

Thus talking to the shrew, and quoting exemplary Petruchio, he packed his clothes carefully in the wagon-bottom, and then — laughing at the ludicrousness of the situation, in spite of himself — stepped cautiously down into the water.

"Aha ! " said he, at the first chill : " I must give my head a plunge, or the blood will rush into it." So he took off his wig and laid it in his hat. Then he ducked himself once or twice. Then he waded to the mare's head, took her gently by the bridle and led her out.

In going up the oozy bank from the water's edge, the animal's plashing hoofs bespattered him with mud from head to foot. He therefore left her on the roadside, and, taking his handkerchief, ran back to wash and dry himself a little before putting on his clothes.

He had cleansed himself of the mud, and was standing on a log beside the bridge, making industrious use of his handkerchief, when he thought he heard a wagon. Fearing to be caught in that most unclerical condition, without even his wig, he looked up hastily over the bridge. There was no wagon coming, but there was one going. It was his own. Queen Bess was deliberately walking away ; for there was a nice sense of justice in that mare, and having refused to start when he wanted her to, it was meet that she should balance that fault by starting when he did not want her to. Poor Dodd had not thought of that.

Taken quite by surprise, and appalled by the horrible possibility that presented itself to his mind, he immediately started in pursuit. Bess had been either too obstinate or too mad to be frightened at the apparition of him in the water, deeming it perhaps a device to make her "go 'long." But now a glimpse of the unfamiliar white object flashing after her was enough, and away she went.

"Now do thy speedy utmost," Dodd! Remember that your clothes are in the buggy; and think not of the stones that bruise your feet. Ah! what a race! But it is unequal, and it is brief. The rascally jockey said too truly, "There's lots of travel in that beast, Parson!" The faster Dodd runs, the more frightened is she; and since he failed at the first dash to grasp the flying vehicle, there is no hope for him. He has lost his breath utterly before she has fairly begun to run. He sees that he may as well stop, and he stops. Broken-winded, asthmatic, gasping, despairing, he stands, a statue of distress (or very much like a statue, indeed), on the roadside, and watches horse and buggy disappearing in the distance. Was ever respectable, middle-aged, slightly corpulent, slightly bald country parson in just such a predicament?

Melissa would certainly look in vain for his coming, that sweet Sunday morning. And who — who would preach for Selwyn

III.

PARSON DODD'S SUNDAY-MORNING CALL.

THE mere loss of horse and buggy was nothing. But O, his clothes! Parson Dodd even hoped to see the vehicle upset or smashed, and his garments, or at least some portion of them, flung out on the roadside. But nothing of the kind occurred, as far as he could see. Of all his fine wardrobe, he had only a handkerchief, — and what is a handkerchief on such an occasion?

Talk of a drowning man's fancies! No thrice-drowned wretch ever suffered anything comparable to Parson Dodd's wild, swift-flashing thoughts, during the brief moments he stood there. He imagined the assembling of the congregation; the waiting and wondering; the arrival perhaps of his punctual clothes and sermon, for they had gone straight forward on the road to the parish; then the alarm, and the whole country roused to search for him.

But there was one subject demanding his immediate attention, — something must be done; and what? He could go to the nearest house and ask for clothes, if he had any clothes to go in! He was reminded of the theological paradox, restated in the very sermon he was to have preached that morning, namely, that, in order to pray for grace, we must have grace to pray. He had wished for a good, practical illustration of his view of that difficulty, and now he had it. Impossible, without clothes, to ask for clothes! Such whimsical fancies will sometimes flit lightly across the mind, even in moments of great distress.

It occurred to him that he might lie in the neighboring woods all day, and then set out for home, ten miles off, under cover of the night. But the hardships of such a course, — twelve hours of nakedness, weariness, famine, — were too appalling. No; something desperate must be done. "I must make a raid for covering of some kind!" thought the unhappy parson.

There was a little low, red-painted dwelling-house in sight, standing well back from the road, with a broad woodshed behind it, and a brown barn behind that. It was flanked by a field of waving rye, — a providential circumstance, the good man thought; it would serve to cover his approach. "I can stand in the rye up to my neck, while I call for help, and explain my situation." So he advanced, wading through the high, nodding grain, which his hands parted before him: a wretched being, but hopeful; and with light fancies still bubbling on the current of his darker reflections.

"Gin a body meet a body coming through the rye," thought he.

A Sunday-morning stillness pervaded farm and dwelling. A quail whistled on the edge of the field, "More wet! more wet!" which sounded to Parson Dodd much like a mocking allusion to his own recent passage of the river. Glossy swallows were twittering about the eaves of the barn; and enviable doves, happy in their feathers, were cooing on the sunny side of the old shed-roof.

In the midst of this scene of perfect rural tranquillity, the barn door was opened. The parson's heart beat fast; somebody was leading out a horse. It was a woman!

A woman with a masculine straw hat on her head. She was followed by another woman, also in a straw hat, bringing a horse-collar. Then came a third woman, similarly covered, carrying a harness. The horse's halter and afterward his head were passed through the collar, which was then turned over on his neck and pressed back against his breast; the harness was put on and buckled; and then, — horrible to tell! — a fourth straw-hatted woman appeared, and held up the shafts of an old one-horse wagon, while the other three backed the animal into them, and hooked the traces.

"My luck!" said the parson, through teeth chattering with excitement, if not with cold. "Not a man on the place! All women! And there's another somewhere. Why did n't I think? It's the house of the Five Sisters!"

The five Misses Wiretop, spinsters, known to all the country round about. They were rather strong-minded, and very strong-bodied; they kept this house, and wore straw hats, and tilled their few ancestral acres, and dispensed with man's assistance (except occasional aid in seed-time and harvest), and went regularly to church, and were very respectable.

"They are getting ready for church now," thought Parson Dodd. "They go to Selwyn's. I always see them there. They are going to hear me preach!"

No doubt they would have been glad to do anything for him that lay in their power; for though they did not think much of men generally, they had a regard for parsons, and for Parson Dodd in particular; he knew that from the serious, reverential glances turned up at him ever from the Five Sisters' pew. "Yet it is n't myself they care for," thought he, "it's my cloth." And here he was without his cloth!

He asked himself, moreover, what they could do for him, even if he should make his wants known to them. Of course there were no male garments in *their* house; and the most he could expect of them was an old lady's gown. He fancied himself in that!

He reasoned, however, that these sisters and their horse might help him to recover his garments and his mare. So he advanced still nearer, and was about calling out to them over the top of the grain, when the Sabbath stillness was broken by a sharp voice, —

"Stop, you sir! Stop, there!"

He did stop, as if he had been shot at. Turning his eyes in the direction of the voice, he saw the fifth sister, with one sleeve of her Sunday gown on, and with one naked arm, leaning her head out of a chamber window, and gesticulating violently.

"Git out o' that rye! git out o' that rye! right straight out! Do you hear, you sir? Do you hear?"

Parson Dodd must have been deaf not to have heard. But how could he obey? Instead of getting out of the rye, he crouched down in it until only the shining top of his bald crown was visible, like a saucer turned up in the sun.

"Madam!" he shouted back, "I beg of you —"

But the sharp voice interrupted him: "Don't you know no better? Can't a poor woman raise her little patch of rye, but some creatur' must come tramp, tramp through it? Don't you know what a path is for? There's the lane; why did n't you come up the lane?"

Poor Dodd would have been only too glad to explain why. But now rose a clamor of female voices, as the four sisters at the barn ran down to the end of the house, between it and the field, to learn what was the matter.

"In the rye!" said the sister at the window, pointing. "Some creatur' tryin' to hide, — don't ye see him? Looks like a man. What ye want? Why don't ye come out? Scroochin' down there! Who be ye, anyhow?"

"Ladies," said poor Dodd, putting up his chin timidly, and looking over the grain with a very piteous expression, "don't you know me?"

But that was a very absurd question. Certainly they did not know him without his wig. Where were those wavy brown locks, which looked so interesting in the preacher's desk, especially to the female portion of his congregation? Could any one be expected to recognize in that shorn and polished pate the noble head and front of the bachelor parson? No, he must proclaim himself.

"Ladies! good friends! don't be alarmed, I entreat. I have met with a —"

He was going to say misfortune. But just then he met with something else, which interrupted him.

The Five Sisters kept, as a protection to their loneliness, a very large dog. One of them, learning that there was a *creatur'* in the rye, had, before learning what that *creatur'* was, whistled for Bruce. Bruce had come. He perceived a rustling, or caught a gleam of the inverted saucer, and made a dash at the field, leaping upon the dilapidated boundary-wall. His deafening yelps from that moment drowned every other sound. He could n't be called off even by her who had set him on. Terror at the sight of a naked man (few sights are more terrifying to an unsophisticated dog) rendered him wholly wild and unmanageable. There he stood on the wall, formidable, bristling with rage and fright, and intercepting every word of the poor, gasping wretch in the grain with his furious barking.

I am very sorry to say that Dodd was about as badly frightened as the dog. He crouched, shrank away, and finally retreated, the brute howling and yelping after him, and the exasperated spinsters screaming to him to take the path, and not trample down the rye, — did n't he know what a path was for?

So ended Parson Dodd's Sunday-morning call on the Five Sisters.

IV.

MR. HILLBRIGHT SETS OFF ON HIS MISSION.

WHEN Mr. Hillbright sent our friend Jervey for the mythical soap, it is by no means certain that he contemplated escaping from the Asylum. I think, if we could hear Hillbright's part of the story, it would be something like this : —

He had detected the turning of the key in the boat-house

locker, and, hastening to it the moment Jervey was gone, had found that his clothes were locked up. What was that for? To prevent him from putting them on, of course, and walking off in his keeper's absence.

"They fear I will walk off, do they? Then I will walk off!"

Such, very probably, was his brief train of reasoning; and such, very certainly, the conclusion arrived at. Should the trifling want of a few rags of clothing stand in the way of a great resolution? Should he who bore the sins of the world, and whose duty it was to go forth and preach and convert the world, neglect such an opening as this to get out and fulfil his mission?

"Providence will clothe me!" And, indeed, it looked as if Providence meant to do something of the kind. "Behold!" There was a long piece of carpet, very ancient and faded, in the bottom of the boat; he pulled it up, wrapped it fantastically about him, and was clad.

He then pushed the boat out into the river, giving it an impulse which sent it across to the opposite shore. Then he leaped out, leaving it adrift on the current. When Mr. Jervey found it below the bend, Mr. Hillbright was already walking, with great dignity, in his improvised blanket, across the skirts of a neighboring woodland, like a sachem in his native wilds.

He had not gone far before he began to experience great tenderness in the soles of his feet. Then by degrees it dawned upon him that the loose ends of the carpet flapping about his calves were but a poor substitute for trousers; and that his attire was, on the whole, imperfect. "Too simple for the age," thought he. Picturesque, but hardly the thing in which to appear and proclaim his mission to a fastidious modern society. Would the world, that refused to tolerate him dressed as a gentleman, accept him

now that he was rigged out more like a king of the Canni-
bal Islands?

He tried various methods of wreathing the folds of an-
tique tapestry about his person; all of which seemed open
to criticism. He was beginning to think Providence might
have done better by him, when, getting over a fence, he
found himself on the public highway.

He knew he would be followed by his friends at the
Asylum; and here he accordingly stopped to take an ob-
servation. He was near the summit of a long hill. At the
foot of it, near half a mile off, he saw a horse coming at a
fast gallop, which to his suspicious mind suggested pursuit,
and he shrank back into some bushes to remain concealed
while it passed.

As the animal ascended the slope, the gallop relaxed to
a leisurely canter, the canter declined to a trot, and, long
before the summit was attained, the trot had become a
walk. The horse had no rider, but there was a buggy at
its heels. Arrived near the spot where Hillbright was hid,
it turned up on the roadside, and put down its head to nip
grass. Then Hillbright saw that there was nobody in the
buggy. The horse was a runaway, that had been stopped
by the long stretch of rising ground. The horse, I may
as well add, was a bay mare.

"Providence is all right," said Hillbright, emerging from
the bushes. "This is for my sore feet."

At sight of the strange figure, grotesque in faded scroll
patterns of flowing tapestry, the mare shied, and would
have got away, but a two-mile course, with a hill at the
end of it, had tamed her spirit. So she merely sprang to
a corner of the fence, and remained an easy capture.

As Hillbright was about setting foot into the vehicle, —
for he had no doubt of its having been sent expressly that
he might ride, — he found an odd heap of things in his

way. There was something that looked like suspenders; and, following up that interesting clew, he drew forth a pair of pantaloons; with them came a coat and waistcoat, all of handsome blue-black cloth. "Providence means that I shall be well clothed," was his happy reflection, as, exploring still further, he discovered boots and underclothes, and a shirt of fine linen, with a wonderfully refulgent ruffled bosom. With a triumphant smile, he proceeded to put the things on, and found them an excellent fit.

There was still a hat left, freighted and ballasted with various valuables, uppermost among which was a luxuriant chestnut-brown wig. Now, Hillbright had never worn a wig. But since he had borne the sins of the world, the top of his head had become bare, and was not here a plain indication that it ought to be covered? He accepted the augury, and put on the wig.

Next came a richly embroidered white neckerchief, for which he also found its appropriate use. Then in the bottom of the hat remained a gold watch, which he cheerfully put into his fob; a plump porte-monnaie which he pocketed with a smile; and a thin package of manuscripts betwixt dainty morocco covers, which, untying its neat pink ribbons, he proceeded to examine.

The miracle was complete. The package was a sermon.

"This is all direct from Heaven!" said Hillbright, delighted, and having no more doubt of the truth of his surmise than if he had seen the buggy and its contents let down in a golden cloud from the sky.

Thinking to find room for the package in the broad breast-pocket of his coat, he discovered an obstacle, which he removed. It proved to be a little oval pocket-mirror. He held it up before him, and had reason to be pleased with the flattering account it gave of himself. The graceful wig, embroidered white cravat, ruffled shirt-bosom, and blue-black suit became him wonderfully well; they made a new man of him.   Had he known Dodd of Coldwater, he would almost have taken himself for that well-got-up bachelor parson.

Then for the hat, which was a stylish black beaver, somewhat the worse for its ride; giving it a little needful polishing before putting it on, he noticed a letter protruding from the lining.   He opened it and read : —

"*Reverend and dear Sir :* — *We have made all the arrangements.   The Ex. is all right.   You preach for Selwyn at Longtrot, on Sunday, the 7th.*   "*B. B.*"

This seemed plain enough to the gratified Hillbright. "We" he understood to mean his unseen friendly guardians.   The "arrangements" they had made were, so far as he could see, excellent; he was provided with everything!   The "Ex." undoubtedly alluded to his *exit* from the Asylum; and that was certainly "all right."   To-day was Sunday, the 7th; and here was his work all laid out for him. .   Who Selwyn was, and where Longtrot was, he did not know; but doubtless it would be revealed.

The signature of the missive puzzled him at first; but soon a happy interpretation occurred to him.   It was evidently no signature at all, but an injunction.   "B. B." stood for "Be! Be!" and it signified, "BE A MAN!   BE A GREAT MAN!   BE THYSELF!   BE HILLBRIGHT!"

Yet when he came to scrutinize the address of the letter, he perceived that the name of Hillbright, against which the world had conceived an unreasonable prejudice, was to be dropped for a season.   "It appears," said he, "I am to be known as Dodd, — E. Dodd, — Rev. E. Dodd.   I don't see what the E. stands for.   I wonder what my first name is?"

So saying, he stepped into the buggy, gathered up the reins from the dasher, put under his feet the carpet that was lately on his back, and set off grandly on his grand mission.

The bay mare was herself again ; she did not balk.

V.

JAKES IN PURSUIT.

AMONG the officers sent out in pursuit of the fugitive from the Asylum was the superintendent of the Asylum farm, a stout, red-faced man, named Jakes, — a brother, by the way, of our friend Colonel Jakes of Coldwater. He took with him an Irish laborer named Collins, also a strong rope with which to bind, and a coarse farmer's suit with which to clothe, the madman when caught.

The superintendent and his man put a horse before a light carryall, and had a fine time driving about on the pleasant country roads, while others of the pursuing party scoured fields and woods on foot: At last they struck the Longtrot road, and turned off toward Coldwater.

They had not driven far in that direction before they saw a man coming in a buggy.

"A minister, ye may know by his white choker," observed Collins.

"You're right, Patrick," said Jakes, "and I vow, I believe I know who he is ! I know that bay mare, anyhow. She's a brute my brother over in Coldwater got shaved on by a travelling jockey ; and he told me last week, with a grin on one side of his face, he had put her off on the minister. I bet my head that's Parson Dodd !

Good morning, sir; beg pardon!" And Superintendent Jakes reined up on the roadside. "Have you seen — have you met — hold on, if you please, sir — a minute!"

Thus appealed to, the stranger stopped his horse. Superintendent Jakes thought that face was somehow familiar, and so thought Collins. In fact, they had seen it more than once about the Asylum grounds, within a few days, as the owner of the said face knew very well. But since one sometimes fails to recognize old friends in strange circumstances, it is no wonder that these farmers did not identify the new patient in Dodd's clothes.

"We 're looking for a crazy man that got away from the Asylum this morning," said Jakes. "A man about five feet nine or ten. Rather portly. Good-looking and gentlemanly when dressed; but he ran off naked. Have you seen or heard of such a man?"

"I have n't seen anybody crazier than you or I," said the supposed parson.

This sounded so much like a joke, though uttered very gravely, that Jakes was tempted to speak of the bay mare.

"I think I know that beast you 're driving. You had her of Colonel Jakes of Coldwater, did n't you? Well, he 's my brother. Your name is Dodd, I believe."

"I have been called Dodd. But can you tell me what my first name is? It begins with E," said the driver of the bay mare, with a shrewd, almost a cunning look, which did not strike Jakes as being very ministerial. Yet he had heard that Dodd was something of a joker.

"I never heard you called anything but Parson Dodd. Yes, I have too. You made a speech at the convention; I read it in the paper. *E* stands for *Ebenezer*."

"Thank you," said the other. "I 'm glad I 've found

out. Thank you,"—smiling, and then suddenly casting his eyes on the ground.

"How do you find the mare?" said Jakes, by way of retort.

"Perfect; arrangements all perfect."

"That so? No bad tricks? Of course she's all right; glad you find her so," grinned Jakes.

"How far is it to Longtrot?" asked the counterfeit Dodd.

"About a mile 'n' a half — two mile — depends upon where in Longtrot you're going."

"Do you know Selwyn?"

"Minister Selwyn, preacher in the yaller meetin'-house? I don't know him, but I know of him. How does she start off?"

"You shall see."

The bay mare started off very well; and the fugitive from the Asylum, having obtained from his pursuer rather more valuable information than he gave in return, disappeared over the crest of the hill, on his way to the "yaller meetin'-house" in Longtrot.

"Wonder if she re'lly ha'n't balked with him yet?" said Superintendent Jakes, as he drove on. "I guess he's a jolly sort of parson. I've seen him somewhere, sure's the world, though I can't remember where."

"You have, and I was there," said Collins; "though where it was, I remember no more than yourself."

They made inquiries for the fugitive all along the route, but could hear of no more extraordinary circumstance, that Sunday morning, than a runaway horse, seen by one or two families, as it passed on the road to Longtrot.

"It must have gone by before we turned the corner," said Jakes, "for we've seen no nag but the parson's."

At last they came in sight of a little red-painted house, standing well back from the street. . "This is the home of

the Five Sisters, Patrick," said Jakes.   "Guess we 'll give
'em a call."

He turned up the lane, driving between the house and
the rye-field, and stopped in front of the wood-shed.   The
dog, still bristling from his recent excitement, gave a surly
bark, and went growling away.   At the same time, five
vivacious female faces appeared, three in the doorway and
two at an open window, and "set up such cackling" (as
Jakes ungallantly expressed it) that he could "hardly hear
himself think."

"Is this Mr. Jakes?" cried one.

"From the Asylum?" cried another.

"I told you so, sister!   I told you so!" cried a third.

"I knowed the man was—" cried a fourth.

"Crazy!" cried the fifth, and all together.

"Dog Bruce chased him out of the rye—"

"Sneaked off behind the fences—"

"Over toward Neighbor Lapham's—"

"An' sister Delia declares—"

"Hush, hush, sister!"

"Yes, I will!   She declares she believes he had n't a
rag o' clothin' to his back!"

"Thank you," said Jakes, having got all the information
he wanted almost without the asking.   "He 's my man!
Thank ye, sisters!   Good morning."

VI.

THE WIDOW GARCEY.

At the bay-window of the pretty Gothic parsonage in
Longtrot sat the widow of the late pastor.   She was
dressed in voluminous black, exceedingly becoming to her

still fresh complexion and to her full style of beauty. If
"sighing and grief" had not produced on her precisely the
effect of which Falstaff complained, it had not certainly
wasted her to a shadow. No wonder if the contemplation
of those generous proportions, of those cheeks still fair and
round, and of the serene temper that served to keep them
so, had persuaded Parson Dodd that there might be something yet left for him in the future better than the lonely
life he was living.

There was a book in the fair hand that had embroidered
the white neckcloth "for her dear husband." It was that
absorbing poem of Pollok's, "The Course of Time," which
she justly deemed not too lively for Sunday reading. Her
serious large eyes were fixed on its pages, except when
ever and anon they glanced restlessly over it, out of the
window and down the pleasant, shady street, as if in ex-
pectation of somebody quite as interesting as the poet
Pollok. Somebody who did *not* make his appearance,
driving down betwixt the overhanging elms, past the
church-green, and up to the gate of the parsonage, as in
fancy she saw him so plainly whenever her eyes were on
the book. Why did they look up at all, since it was only
to refute the pretty vision?

Poor Melissa sat there until she seemed living the
Course of Time, instead of reading it. Occasionally she
varied the direction of her glances by looking at her
watch; and she grew more and more troubled as she saw
the hour slipping irrevocably by which the husband's
friend should have given to comforting the fatherless and
widow that Sunday morning.

"What can have happened?" she asked herself. "He
must have taken offence at something! What have I said
or done? It must be the cravat! Why did I do so fool-
ish a thing as to send it with a note?" She could have

said what she wished to say so much better than she could write it !

The first bell rang. And now people were going to church. The children were teasing to start. They were tired of sitting still in the house. What was she waiting for ? Was that old Dodd coming again to-day ?

" Levi ! never let me hear you call him *old Dodd* again ! Mr. Dodd is still a young man, and he has been a good friend to your poor mother. There ! " she exclaimed, with a little start, for her eyes, wandering down the street again, saw the long-expected buggy coming at last.

It was a peculiar buggy, high in the springs, and with a high and narrow top. She could not mistake it. She was equally sure of the stylish hat and wavy brown locks and ample shirt-frill of the driver. But in an instant the thrill of hope the sight inspired changed to a chill of disappointment and dismay. Parson Dodd did not drive on to the parsonage, as he had always done before, when coming to preach for Selwyn. The buggy turned up to the meeting-house, and disappeared in the direction of the horse-sheds.

She waited awhile, in deep distress of mind, to see it or its owner reappear ; but in vain.

" Levi," she said, " go right over to the church, and see if Mr. Dodd has come. Go as quick as you can, but don't let anybody know I sent you."

It seemed to her that the boy was never so provokingly slow in executing an errand.

At last she saw him returning leisurely, watching the orioles in the elms, while her heart was bursting with impatience. She signalled him from the window, and lifted interrogating brows at him. Levi grinned and nodded vivaciously in reply. Yes, the minister had come.

" Are you — are you very sure ? " she tremblingly inquired, meeting him at the door.

"A'n't I!" said the lad. "Did n't I first go and look at his buggy under the shed? He's got a new horse; but I guess I ought to know that buggy, often as it's been in our barn. Then I peeked in through the door, and saw him just going up into the desk."

Poor Mrs. Garcey was now quite ready to go to church. Since Dodd would not come to her, she must go to him; she must see his face, and get one look from him, even if across the space that separated pulpit from pew.

"How was he looking, Levi?" she asked.

"Kind o' queer. I always thought Dodd felt big enough, but I never saw him carry his head quite so high. Looked as if he was mad at something."

"O, I must have offended him!" sighed the unhappy Melissa, putting on her things.

With slow and decorous steps she marshalled forth her little tribe from the gate of the parsonage across the green to the church-porch. The bell was ringing again, its brown back just visible in the high belfry, tumbling and rolling like a porpoise in the waves of its own sound. Wagons were arriving, and the usual throng of church-goers were alighting on the platform or walking up the steps. In the vestibule she found a group of friends inquiring seriously concerning each other's health, and in suppressed voices talking of the latest news. There seemed to be some excitement with regard to an insane man who had that morning escaped from the Asylum, whom nobody appeared to have seen, though he had been heard of by several through those who were out in pursuit of him. Somehow, Melissa took not much interest in the greetings and the gossip of these worthy people, and parting from them, she passed on into the aisle.

"Poor dear! She can't forgit *him*," whispered kind-hearted Mrs. Allgood, with a tear of sympathy gathering

in the eye that followed the gloomily draped and pensive
figure.

"Huh! she's thinkin' of another husband a'ready!"
answered sharp-tongued Miss Lynx, with a toss.

It cannot be denied that of the two, Miss Lynx had the
clearer perception of the hard fact in the case. Yet as she
set it forth, unclothed by grace and the warm tissues of
human sympathy, it was no more the truth than a skeleton
is a living body; and Mrs. Allgood's gentler judgment
was more just. Melissa had not forgotten that good man,
Garecy; and if now, in her loneliness and bereavement,
she cherished hope of other companionship, was it for
tart Miss Lynx to condemn her? Nay, who, without
knowledge of the human heart, and compassion for its suf-
ferings and its needs, had even a right to judge her?

She passed down the aisle, preceded by her little ones
(the elder of whom, by the way, were beginning to be not
so very little), and followed them into the pew in which she
had first sat when a bride. She would have been alone in
it then, but for the two or three poor persons to whom
she was always glad to give seats. But one after another
a little Garecy had appeared, first in her arms, perhaps,
then in the seat beside her, and thus, year by year, the
family row had increased, until now it almost filled the
cushioned slip. A mist of tender, regretful sentiment
seemed to suffuse the very atmosphere about her as she
listened to the tone of the bell, and thought what changes
had come over her dream of life since she first sat there
and looked up with pride to see the beloved, the eloquent
— *her* Garecy — in the desk! Now, here she was again,
looking with anxious eyes and a troubled heart for another.

There were the well-known wavy chestnut-brown locks,
and a shoulder of the blue-black coat, just visible from the

15 *

side-slip in which she sat. But the wearer did not once deign to look at her. He held his head bowed behind the desk, as if in devout contemplation, and thoughts in which she, alas! had no share. She longed to see him lift it, and turn toward her those gracious, sympathizing features, the very sight of which was a comfort to her heart. And it must be confessed she had a strong curiosity regarding the embroidered cravat.

"I must speak with him after the service," thought she. "I will make him come to the house." And she turned and whispered to the topmost head of the little row.

"It has just occurred to me, Levi, you'd better go and put his horse in our barn. It will be too bad to have the poor beast standing under the shed all day."

"'T won't hurt anything; besides, he might have drove over there himself, if he wanted his horse put out," said Levi, with a scowl.

"You can get into the buggy and ride over," said his mother, grown all at once wonderfully solicitous with regard to the welfare of the poor beast.

The ride was an object, and Levi went.

The bell stopped ringing, the choir ceased singing, the congregation was in its place, all hushed and expectant; and still Levi did not return. His mother would have felt anxious about him at any other time; but now a greater trouble absorbed the less.

It was not like Parson Dodd to sit so long in that way with his head down. A movement of the arm, and a rustle of leaves heard in the stillness of the house, showed that he was turning over the manuscript of his sermon, or selecting hymns, or looking up chapter and verse. But all that should have been done before. He ought not now to keep the people waiting.

The silence was broken by a cough. This was followed

by several coughs, which appeared to have been hitherto suppressed. Then entered four of the Five Sisters, uncommonly late this morning, for some reason. In spite of untoward circumstances, they had come to hear Mr. Dodd — that dear, good man — preach. And now a buzz of whispers began to run through the congregation ; hushed, however, as soon as the preacher rose.

Melissa, watching intently, saw the noble head of luxuriant chestnut-brown hair slowly lifted. Then bloomed the abundant shirt-ruffle over the desk, together with — yes, the white neckerchief embroidered by her own hand ! But even while she recognized it, a thrill of amazement, a chill of consternation, passed over her, as the wearer, stretching forth his hands, cried out in a loud, strange voice, —

" We will pray for the sins of the world ! "

VII.

FARMER LAPHAM'S EXPLOIT.

WHEN Parson Dodd withdrew from the society of the Five Sisters and their dog Bruce, he descried across the fields a house and barn situated on another road, and made toward them, under the shelter of walls and fences, thinking that if he could take them in the rear, and enter the barn unperceived, he might at least secure a horse-blanket in which to introduce himself to the family.

He found, however, to his dismay, that they must be finally approached across a range of barren pasture, unsheltered even by a shrub. No friendly rye-field here; and he was too far off to make known his wants by shouting. He did shout two or three times from behind an old cow-house in which he took refuge, but timidly, and without the desired effect. What was to be done ?

He had turned aside to visit the cow-house, in the feeble hope of finding there some relief to his forlorn condition. But it was empty even of straw.

As he cast about him in his despair, seeking for something wherewith to cover his farther advance, his eye fell upon the cow-house door. " If I only had that off its hinges, I might carry it before me," thought he. He took hold of it and found it could be easily removed. In a minute he had it in his arms. "Samson carrying off the gates of Gaza !" was the lively comparison that occurred to him, — but with this difference : whereas, in familiar Bible pictures, the strong man was represented as bearing his burden on his back, this modern Samson poised his upon his portly bosom. "Circumstances alter cases," thought he.

With arms stretched across it, grasping its edges with his hands, and just lifting it from the ground (it was not very heavy), he moved forward with it cautiously, — much like a Roman soldier under cover of his immense *scutum*, or door-shaped shield, occasionally setting it down to rest (being careful at such times to take his toes from under it), or reconnoitring his ground from behind it ; but always keeping it skilfully betwixt his person and the enemy's walls.

Now, one can easily picture the amazement of the worthy Lapham family, when its younger members reported a wonderful phenomenon in the cow-pasture, that calm Sunday morning ; and mother and children running to look, behold ! there was the cow-house door advancing in this extraordinary manner to pay them a visit ; staggering slightly, and balancing itself occasionally on its lower cor-

ners, like a door that had as yet learned but imperfectly
the art of walking! Close scrutiny might perhaps have
revealed to them the human fingers clasping the edges of
it; or the feet of flesh and blood taking short steps under
it; or the glistening crown of the bearer peeping furtively
from behind. But when the vulgar mind is greatly astonished, it is prone to see only that which most astonishes;
and, accordingly, good Mrs. Lapham and the little Laphams, failing to discriminate in such trifling matters as
hands and feet, saw only the gross phenomenon of the
perambulating door. It was like Birnam Wood coming to
Dunsinane.

What gave a sort of dramatic effect to the apparition
was the grotesque outline of a human figure, large as life,
which the boys had chalked on the outside of the door, for
a target. As soon as they saw this advance, grinning at
them, they were greatly excited; and one ran for the
gun.

"Keep back, mother!" said he; "I'll give the old
thing a shot, if 't is Sunday!"

"Stop! You sha' n't, Jason! Martin, run for your
father! Run!"

Mr. Lapham had been talking with a stranger at the
gate, who had just driven up when the children ran out to
proclaim the wonder.

"Nonsense, children!" said he. "A door don't move
across the country without somebody to help it; you ought
to know that, mother. Wal! there!" he exclaimed, wit-
nessing the miracle from the kitchen window. "It is on
its travels, sure enough! Jason, run and see if you can
catch that man I was talking with. Holler! scream! Be
quick!"

"Who is he, father?" asked mother.

"A man from the Asylum — says one of their crazy folks

got away this morning. Run off without his clothes. He's behind that door, I 'll bet a dollar!"

This seemed a very plausible explanation of the mystery; but it did not serve to tranquillize the mother and children. Was not a live madman as much to be dreaded as a walking door?

"Don't be frightened. Just shet the house and keep dark. I 'll head him off. Give me the gun, I may want it." And arming himself, out the farmer sallied.

Parson Dodd had by this time perceived that his approach was creating a sensation. For want of a pocket, he had tied his handkerchief to his wrist. He now fluttered that white flag over a corner of the door for a signal; then, with his hand behind his mouth for a trumpet, summoned a parley. Looking to see some friendly recognition of his flag of truce, great was his consternation at beholding so warlike a demonstration as a man running to the ambush of some quince-bushes with a gun. In vain he fluttered his white flag, and called for help.

"I a'n't goin' to fall into no trap sot by a crazy pate!" thought shrewd Farmer Lapham, as he concealed himself.

Poor Dodd was in a terrible situation. He could not advance without the risk of receiving a bullet; neither could he lay the door down, unless, indeed, he first laid himself down, and then drew it over him for a blanket. He might retreat, but that movement, too, presented difficulties. So there he stood, holding up the target, beckoning and shouting himself hoarse to no purpose.

And now the musical clamor of church bells rose on the tranquil morning air. "*The wedding-guest here beat his breast, for he heard the loud bassoon!*" thought he; for still he could not keep odd fancies out of his brain. Yet how far off those bells sounded! — not in distance only; they seemed to be in a world of which he had once dreamed.

He thought of the sermon he was to have preached that day as something he might have written in a previous state of existence, something quite foreign to the dread realities of life.

"I can't stand here holding up a door forever!" thought he at last. And he determined to move on, in spite of bullets. So he took up the door, and resumed his march.

Observing the point he was aiming at, Lapham thought it wise to get into the barn before him, and station himself where he could keep guard over his property, watch the supposed madman, and fire a defensive shot if necessary.

Dodd, bearing up the door, did not perceive this flank movement; but advancing to within a few yards of the barn, he was astonished at hearing a voice thunder forth from a window, "Stop, or I'll shoot!"

Dodd stopped and peeped forth from behind his portable screen, showing a bald crown which was very much against him.

"His keeper said he was bald on top of his head," the farmer reasoned. And he called out, "What do you want?"

"*Rest and a guide and food and fire*," was running in Dodd's mind; but he answered in plain prose, and very emphatically, "I want clothes."

This was another corroborating circumstance, and a very strong one.

"How came you here without clothes?"

"I lost them by a singular accident. I am a clergyman, on my way to preach."

This was conclusive. "The very chap! His keeper said he imagined himself a preacher," thought the farmer. "Wonder if I can't manage to trap him!" And he cast about him for the means.

"I'll explain everything; only give me something to cover myself, and don't keep me standing here!" said Parson Dodd, growing impatient.

By this time Lapham had formed his plan. "Do just as I tell ye now, and you shall have clothes. Come into the barn, turn to the right, and you'll find a harness-room, and in it you'll find a frock and overalls. Do you hear?"

Dodd heard, and the prospect of even so poor a covering thrilled his heart with gratitude. He came on with his door, left it leaning against the barn, and entered.

He found the harness-room as described, and seized eagerly upon the frock and overalls. But just as he was putting them on the door of the room flew together with a bang; the crafty farmer, who had hidden behind it, sprang and turned the key, and the "madman" was locked in.

Having accomplished this daring feat, Farmer Lapham, deaf to the cries of his victim, ran out excitedly to call for help, just as Patrick Collins was taking down a pair of bars on the other side of the pasture for Superintendent Jakes to drive through. Their errand was soon made known.

"I've ketched the feller for ye!" cried the elated farmer. And he led Jakes to the dungeon within which the entrapped parson was calling lustily.

"Unlock the door; don't be afraid, man!" said Jakes.

Lapham opened it and stepped cautiously back while the superintendent entered, followed by Collins with a rope and a bundle of clothes.

Within stood the captive, a comical figure, in loose blue frock and overalls, barefoot and wigless, and with a countenance in which indignation at the farmer, joy at the prospect of deliverance, and a consciousness of his own ludicrous situation, were mingled in an expression which was very droll indeed.

"How are you?" said Jakes in an offhand way.   "We have brought your clothes; would you like to put 'em on?"

"I would; and I am infinitely obliged to you, my good friends!" said poor Dodd, thinking the worst of his troubles now over.   "How did you find — But what — These — these are not my clothes!"

"A'n't they?" said Jakes.   "You'd better put 'em on, though.   They'll do till you get back to the doctor's."

"To the doctor's?   What do you mean?   I am a clergyman.   I was on my way to preach — "

"Yes, we understand all about that.   Come, on with the clothes.   We don't expect you'll give us any trouble, Mr. Hillbright."

"Hillbright!   I am Dodd, — Dodd of Coldwater, — a minister!"

"There are two of you, then!" said Jakes, laughing incredulously.   "We just met *one* Parson Dodd, in his buggy, driving the bay mare he had of my brother, going over to preach at Longtrot.   He's there by this time."

"Dodd — Longtrot — the bay mare!" gasped out the astonished parson.   "Impossible!"

"Come, no nonsense, Mr. Hillbright!   Colonel Jakes, of Coldwater, is my brother, and I know the mare perfectly well, — the balky brute!"

"There is some mistake here, Mr. Jakes, — if that is your name.   I knew the Colonel had a brother at the Insane Asylum, and I suspect you are he."

"Yes, and you've seen me there often enough, I suppose.   Now, no more fooling.   I don't want to use force, if it can be avoided; but you must go with us, — that's all there is about it.   Collins, pass along that rope."

"Never mind the rope," said Dodd.   "Just hear my explanation, and you'll save yourself and me some trouble. That mare balked with me in the middle of the river, and to lead her out I had to take off my clothes and put them in the wagon, and she ran away with them."

"A very ingenious story," said Jakes; "but you would n't have thought on 't if I had n't just said she was a balky brute. Come, this won't do. Mr. Hillbright, or Mr. Dodd, or whatever your name, you must go with us; and you can take your choice, whether to go peaceably or be tied with this rope. We're much obliged to you, Mr. Lapham."

Seeing resistance to be vain, Parson Dodd stepped into the wagon, stared at by the whole family of Laphams, who had come out to get a view of the madman, and was carried off triumphantly by Jakes and Collins.

VIII.

DÉNOUEMENT.

ANIMATED by the prospect of a ride, young Levi Garcey backed the minister's buggy out from under the shed, got up into it, took the reins, and was having his simple reward, when, as he was crossing the street, a slight misunderstanding occurred between him and the bay mare. She wanted to return homeward, never yet having enjoyed the hospitalities of the Garcey stable. Not being permitted to follow her own sweet will, she refused to move at all, — balked, in short. And this was the reason why Levi did not go back into church.

There he was in the middle of the street, when a man in a chaise drove up. He was the same who had stopped at Farmer Lapham's gate, and whom Jason Lapham had failed to overtake. To be more explicit, it was Jervey.

Stopping to help the boy out of his trouble, or to make inquiries concerning Hillbright, he remarked in the bottom of the buggy something that had a familiar look. He pulled it up, and recognized the strip of carpet belonging to the doctor's boat.

"How came this thing here?"

"I d'n' know. I found it in the buggy."

"Whose buggy is it?"

"The minister's, — Mr. Dodd's."

"Where is he?"

"In the meetin'-house, where I ought to be," said Levi.

"Just look out for my horse a minute," said Jervey. And he started for the church door, rightly regarding the carpet as a clew which might lead to something.

What it did lead to was the most astonishing thing that ever happened in all his remarkable experience. He had thought that, if he could get a word with the minister, he might perhaps hear from Hillbright, and lo! the minister was Hillbright himself! He did not recognize him at first in that wonderful costume, which seemed little short of miraculous; and he could scarcely credit his senses when the madman's phraseology and tones of voice (he was still praying at a furious rate for the sins of the world) betrayed his identity.

The prayer was an incoherent outpouring of mingled sense and nonsense; and the congregation was beginning to show marked signs of uneasiness and excitement under it.

"What's up?" whispered Jervey to the sexton.

"I don't know," replied the sexton. "We expected Dodd of Coldwater to preach to-day. But he seems to have sent an odd genius in his place, — in his clothes, too."

"Can we get into the pulpit without going through the aisle?" Jervey quietly asked.

" Yes, I can show you.   What under the sun is the matter ? "

" Your odd genius is a madman, that escaped this morning, naked, from the Asylum."

" 'T a'n't possible !   He came in Dodd's buggy ! "

" Then I am afraid some mischief has happened to Dodd."

" A madman ! — naked !   He must have murdered Dodd
for his clothes ! "

" Keep quiet.   Don't alarm the people ; but just call out
two or three of your prominent men."

I know not how many in the congregation had by this
time learned the real character of the man who appeared before them so strangely in Dodd's place and in Dodd's attire.
It had taken some a good while to find out that it was not
Dodd himself.   But there was one who at the first moment
saw the astounding change and feared the worst.

This was Melissa.   She remembered the gossip in the
vestibule concerning the escaped madman, and, connecting
that with the arrival of Dodd's buggy and characteristic
apparel, what else could she infer than that he had been
waylaid and robbed, and perhaps killed ?   The fanatical
extravagance of the prayer corroborated her suspicions.
She glanced around and saw the grave deacons looking
restless and disturbed.   Then came a stranger to the door,
and whispered to the sexton, who whispered to Deacon
Sturgis and Deacon Adams and Dr. Cole, who got up and
went out.

Next came a singular movement in the pulpit.   It was
at the close of the prayer, when the usurper of Dodd's
raiment unclosed his eyes, and, looking about him, saw two
or three men in the shadow of the pulpit stairs.   He
stooped to speak with them ; there was a sound of quick,
low voices ; then the spurious Dodd had disappeared ; and
lo ! there was good Deacon Sturgis standing in front of

the pulpit. The whole congregation was by this time in a rustle of commotion.

"I hope the friends won't be disturbed at all," said he. "A mistake of some little importance has occurred; but everything will come out right, we trust. Meanwhile the services will go on."

Here the deacon read, with great deliberation, the longest hymn he could select. "Congregation will please jine with the choir in singin'," he said; and set the example, in a loud, nasal voice.

The singing ended, he read a passage of Scripture; then called on one of the brethren noted for having a gift that way to offer up a prayer. The prayer too was a long one. Then Deacon Sturgis read another hymn; during the singing of which Deacon Adams came in and whispered a word in his ear.

The second hymn ended, Melissa was watching in great distress of mind to see what the deacons would do, when she noticed all eyes turned again toward the pulpit. Turning hers in the same direction, she barely suppressed a scream; for there, behind the desk, appeared once more the well-known wig, effulgent shirt-ruffle, and blue-black suit. But it was no longer the spurious Dodd that was there. It was Parson Dodd himself!

Riding away with his captors in the carryall, Dodd had rendered so straightforward an account of himself, corroborating it with many particulars concerning Jakes's brother, the Colonel, that Jakes was staggered by it.

"Patrick," said he, aside to Collins, "a'n't it just possible the other Dodd is the man? You know we thought we had seen him before!"

"Ah! but they 're cunning divils! Don't ye belaive a word this feller says," replied Collins.

Jakes, however, was secretly persuaded of his blunder; and he so far deferred to the wishes of his prisoner as to drive over toward Longtrot in pursuit of "the other Dodd." So it happened that the real Dodd's capture as a madman resulted to his advantage, since it hastened the *dénouement* of his unhappy adventure, and enabled him, after all, to preach for Selwyn.

The *dénouement* took place in front of the meeting-house, where Levi was still holding Jervey's horse; where two men, seated in Dodd's buggy, were just starting in search of the owner, — or, rather, trying to start, for the bay mare had something to say about that; and where Patrick, catching a glimpse of Jervey coming out of the vestry with *his* madman, called to him, "Jervey, Jervey! we've got the feller!"

"So have I!" cried Jervey; and there the genuine parson was brought face to face with the counterfeit.

"Gentlemen," said Hillbright, bowing low in his borrowed plumage, "I succumb; I see the world is against me; I must still groan under the sins of it!"

"I owe you a thousand apologies, Mr. Dodd!" said Jakes.

"On the contrary," replied Dodd, having fully recovered his good-humor, "you have done me a service, though it did seem to me one while that — what with you and your Irishman, and your brother and his bay mare — the Jakes family was bound to ruin me."

"Step right into my house, friends!" said Deacon Adams. "There everything can be arranged."

And there everything was arranged, to the satisfaction of everybody, excepting perhaps Hillbright, who was reluctant to put off his Heaven-sent apparel and return to the Asylum without fulfilling his great mission.

Parson Dodd was himself again when he appeared in the

desk ; and it is said that he preached for Selwyn that day
one of his very best sermons

"What a beautiful discourse !" said one of the Five Sisters, thanking him for it as he was going out of church.

"And, only think, sisters," said another of them, "how
near we come to missin' it, all on account of that dreadful
crazy man !   I hope his keepers have got him safe !"

"I hope they have !" said Parson Dodd, dryly, as he
walked out with Melissa, and went over to lunch at the
parsonage.

The joke was out before the afternoon services began ;
and when Dodd reappeared in the desk, it was with difficulty that either he or the gravest of his hearers repressed
a very strong inclination to smile.

The news of his mishap reached Coldwater before he
did ; Superintendent Jakes — to atone for his blunder, I
suppose — having ridden over that afternoon to remon-
strate with his brother, the Colonel, for putting off on the
parson so vicious a brute as the bay mare.   The whole
thing struck the Colonel as so good a joke, and put him
into such excellent humor, that he voluntarily drove the
old gray over to Dodd's the next morning, and offered to
swap back, which offer was most cheerfully accepted by
the parson.   "Did n't I tell ye," said Jakes, "that the
creatur' was always poorest at the start?"   So Dodd got
back his old gray, and somebody else got shaved on the
bay mare.

Parson Dodd continued to travel occasionally the Longtrot road, both on Sunday mornings and week-day after-
noons, until after his marriage.   But now Melissa and the
children (he is remarkably fond of children) make his home
so delightful to him that he leaves it as seldom as possible.
And so it happens that of late years he very rarely goes
over to preach for Selwyn.